DEEP FREEWRITING

How to Masterfully Navigate the creative Flow

STEPHEN LLOYD WEBBER

Apollo Star

Published by APOLLO STAR
apollostarbooks.com

An imprint of Publications Publishing LLC
1603 Capitol Ave
Suite 310 A147
Cheyenne WY 82001
(307) 222-6967, (307) 365-6456 (FAX)

Table of Contents

How to Use This Book

Treat this book like a course. Start at the beginning and move forward only after doing each exercise.

Everything in this book is here to help you make positive shifts with your writing. The key to making this happen is to ensure that you apply what is covered here. The material really becomes yours not from reading it but by experiencing results firsthand.

There are seven core modules. Try to spend an equal amount of time on each. A week per module, for example.

The first module is about dispensing with limiting beliefs, introducing key concepts and getting your feet wet.

The second module introduces some pivotal techniques that make your freewriting more organized and well-structured.

Module three brings in the importance of time, perspective, and the power of questions.

Module four is packed with different exercises and is all about diving into new possibilities, embracing the chaos of creation to get new ideas, explore voice, realize your goals, and how to shift modes to comfortably write for longer durations.

Module five delivers the main event, the heart of it all: the writing marathon. Along with that, there are a host of techniques and tweaks that will help you navigate the flow with ease.

Module six brings in the issue of revision and brings some key distinctions to make this phase of the writing process productive, fun, and creative.

Module seven is about reflection and offers additional strategies to further integrate depth freewriting into your life. It includes some writing recipes you can use depending on what you would like to write and how much time you have.

That's the intended order, but nothing is set in stone. If you feel like skipping around, go for it. And if you have questions about anything or want one-on-one guidance, feel free to reach out to me at stephenlloydwebber.com

Module 1: Flow

Why A New Method?

The pace of life has quickened. We are surrounded by interruptions and demands for attention.

It's time to reclaim command of our creative time. Unless we embrace a more streamlined way to write, our best work will remain unwritten.

To get better, we need to go deeper.

Most of the time people spend writing is time wasted deliberating, procrastinating, and fighting with themselves.

As an English professor, I saw this inner struggle all the time when students took a written test. Despite the fact that I had taught freewriting to all of my students, not all of them kept up with it.

Some students really embraced freewriting and were able to write with no delays. They simply read their test questions and began to write. No head scratching, no chewing their pencil erasers. They had confidence. They didn't need to stare at the page, because they knew the page wasn't going to have the answers on it until they wrote them there.

So what about the rest of the students? They followed a common style of writing I call the "blank stare" style. As a result, it took them a lot longer to finish writing, and on average, the wording of their essays did not flow as smoothly as those written by the students who finished first.

The students who wrote fast were able to get into a flow. The other students never got into a flow, because they were blocked up about trying to get the right ideas on the page.

I'm not going to say that hesitation is wrong, or that if someone needs to stop and think it means they don't know what they're doing. I definitely don't mean that. I'm also not passing judgment against people who write slowly.

I'm sharing what I saw because it lays out a pattern I believe can make all the difference for those who want to write better, faster and more authentically.

The pattern I noticed was that in any given classroom full of writers, those who really embraced what I taught them about freewriting were able to consistently outperform the others.

The freewriters were not necessarily smarter than the writers who insisted on stopping to think. But they certainly showed greater confidence and flow when it came to completing their written exam.

Maybe you can relate to this. Confidence goes hand-in-hand with being in the flow state.

As a contrast, if you think back to moments when you felt blocked, when you stared dully at the blank page, fearful of saying something wrong, those weren't exactly your life's most confident moments. I can relate. It's hard to feel confident while losing a fight with yourself.

A freewriter's confidence is a byproduct of an unblocked writing process. The more you embrace freewriting and use the technique to really go deep, the more you are able to trust your ability to write whenever you need to write something.

It's a simple technique with many diverse applications. It's also easy to learn.

Winning the Fight

Anyone who can write can freewrite, so why don't they? Why do people choose a writing method that makes them feel blocked and keeps them staring at their screens and fighting with themselves?

I don't think fighting with yourself is the path to greatness. When every word is a struggle, I don't think you're likely to be penning the next bestseller.

My experience has shown me that the regular practice of deep freewriting is the quickest way to form a winning relationship with writing. Deep freewriting is a versatile practice. Writers can use it to write better, to write faster, and to connect with their innate voice.

Freewriting in some form or another has been around for a long time, and the simple methods many people are already aware of generally work pretty well. But few people really push the technique to reap the biggest rewards from it.

Even though freewriting is simple, it has amazing depth and nuance to it. My advice is to push it by using the techniques I lay out in this book. There are ways of focusing a freewriting session to go from rough idea to finished draft in a very short time. You can make it work with any form of writing, whether creative, technical, for self-discovery, or to help get your point across to a potential client.

Simply by commiting to write without stopping, you are already well ahead of the curve. Most of the time people spend writing is time wasted deliberating and fighting with their own emotions, their inner critic, their own process. Likewise, much of the struggle with revision comes from frustration and confusion trying to wrestle their language and decipher their own meaning.

Take it from me. I have had my share of struggles as a writer. For many years, my writing process was way slower than it needed to be. I'm no different than the average Joe in this regard. Actually, I may have even been slower than the average Joe, because I over-thought everything. It was only when I truly embraced freewriting by doing several particularly prolonged sessions (several hours to an entire day) that I was able to steamroll past my old blocks for good. I unlearned all sorts of bad habits, and once I finally deconstructed these bad habits, they never came back.

Comfortably freewriting for longer and longer durations is something we will cover in this book.

I want to share these freewriting techniques because I am crazy enough to believe that if more people are aware of them, I can help the world become a better place. Unblocked people can be more creative, innovative, and impactful. Unblocked people can become more of who they really are.

In my opinion, some of the best qualities a writer can have are as follows:

- They have confidence in their ability.
- They feel good when they write.
- They are able to maintain a clear perspective, a larger sense of what they are working on.
- They engage the flow without stopping.

The main focus of this course will be on that last point.

A writer is able to write without stopping because:

- They know enough about what is required of them and they have a good idea of what they have chosen to say, or
- They plainly decide to write without stopping, no matter what.

When a writer uses freewriting to carve a clear path for their language, the time spent writing is just the time it takes to actually put the letters on the page. Their thoughts and emotions are in sync with the flow of their language.

There are plenty of ways of becoming a better writer, but only a few ways that will not only make you a better writer but also a more effortless writer. That means ditching the following:

- writer's block
- muddled writing
- wasted time sitting and thinking of what you need to say next

All of these will be addressed through learning the freewriting techniques I share here.

Now, a word of warning to you. You have to apply what you learn, otherwise it doesn't work! You have to put in the effort. Maybe that part doesn't sound sexy, but the best way to learn something is to practice. And freewriting is exactly the kind of practice worth mastering.

What you practice, you get good at. And because freewriting requires that you adopt an attitude that affirms the creative process, you move towards a writing style that is good at being creative.

Freewriting teaches us to affirm rather than reject mistakes. As a freewriter, not only is it OK if you make a mistake, it's fantastic. Mistakes mean you're fueled, you're moving forward, you're alive, you're working, you trust that you can fine-tune as you go. As freewriters, our constant forward momentum proves that we're good enough, that we can keep going no matter what wildness emerges, no matter what craziness happens.

It's also OK if you don't know exactly what you're writing all the time. Not knowing does not mean failure, and you don't need to stop what you're doing and stare at the blank page for an hour. Trust me, I have tried that. It doesn't guarantee perfection. It just makes writing scarce. With the right technique and the right attitude, writing without stopping even when you don't know what to say gives you the opportunity to discover the best ideas.

"Stop and stare" writers get worried when their drafts get messy. They have the arrogance to expect it all to come out perfectly the first time. That gets them blocked up. Again, I'm speaking from experience here.

I don't mean to suggest that you shouldn't strive for perfection. What I am suggesting is that you reserve this expectation for certain windows of time when it won't interfere with you producing words. Perfectionism is not a problem as long as you choose when to engage your inner critic. First make a mess, then clean it up. If you make a huge mess in your draft, you can invite your perfectionist to come in later and make you look good.

When you're freewriting, the idea is to be freely writing. To find ways of allowing it to be enjoyable. If you're doing it right, then at times it will feel like downright indulgence. More and more, you learn to actually trust the process and be fueled by how satisfying it is. You'll be more sustainably productive this way.

Setting aside the need for things to be perfect can actually be the most direct path to begin improving the quality of your writing. I'll say it again: insisting on perfection doesn't make things any better. It only makes them more rare. Perfectionism during the writing process is fertilizer for excuses that only engender stagnation.

It is UNTRUE that writing needs to feel like hard work.

I'm definitely not denying that writing can be difficult. As someone who has written novels and poems and reviews and articles and essays, I am aware of this. Writing is not automatically pure bliss from beginning to end. However...

It is UNTRUE that you need to stop and think and stare at your screen to earn your Eureka moment.

In most cases, when you adopt the write-and-stop method (heavy on the stop), you aren't interrupted by Eureka-class lightening strikes of inspiration very often. You plod forward, you make mistakes, you stop and think. This kind of writing is as exhausting as hauling a heavy cart up a hill.

Because it's fatiguing rather than replenishing, the longer you persist in a stop-and-think writing session, the less likely any good ideas will emerge.

With deep freewriting, you can write for hours and walk away from your work and feel good. Energized. Curious. Ready for more. The more you freewrite, the more you get in touch with yourself, your own voice, your own nuances of thinking. I have embraced this process for many years and it continues to impress me with all that it has to offer.

Overview of the Traditional Way to Freewrite

If you haven't already heard of him, let me recommend him now: Peter Elbow was absolutely brilliant with sharing his wisdom about freewriting. His expertise around freewriting has entered common knowledge to such an extent that I could have saved myself a lot of time and effort if I had read his book at a younger age. When I did finally get around to reading *Writing Without Teachers*, I was surprised to find that he had already come up with many ideas that I had worked to develop myself from my experience and my discussions with other writers. He didn't invent the freewriting technique, but as far as I am concerned he did more than anyone to popularize and perfect freewriting and bring it into classrooms and businesses and the personal lives of many writers. His books are an excellent place to look if you want to continue your study of freewriting.

Fundamentally, traditional freewriting is writing without stopping for a duration of time. When you freewrite, you engage a certain mode, meaning that you choose to engage with the written word in an intentional way. There are basically two modes: creating and critiquing. When you freewrite, you hold yourself to creating, holding off any critiquing for later.

Both creating and critiquing are good. Both are necessary. And you can be way more effective as a writer if you hold yourself to one mode at a time.

While freewriting itself is basic and easy to understand, there are all sorts of ways of applying and tweaking the technique. The positive potential of mastering freewriting is without limit.

Benefits of Freewriting

- Freewriting is magical. Where before there was nothing, behold! There is now something.

- It breaks writer's block.
- It engages a natural part of you (the creative) that otherwise gets oppressed by the critical mode.
- It establishes a healthy relationship with writing.
- It forms a habit of productivity.
- It deconditions judgmental baggage from English class and elsewhere. Grammatical correctness has its purpose, but let's face it: it'll never be the life of the party. The creator is the life of the party. So, during the first phase of a freewrite, have a party. Then, after the party is done, invite your critical perfectionist to clean up the place and get your writing to shine with correct grammar and usage. That's what the critical perfectionist is good at. Everybody's happy. It's a win-win.
- It allows you to let go of the urge to be locked into your outcome before setting out on the voyage. In this way, you are invited to see chaos not as a threat but an adventure. Chaos is the vital element to construction.
- If you insist that you need to know in advance everything you're going to say, you disallow mystery and discovery. The reality is you can never know everything about something in advance. Writing is a performance if you let it be. Throw your presence into it and see what happens.
- It removes the limits from what you thought possible. This is especially true with the writing marathon. The imagination, chaos, the realms of creativity, they are boundless.
- It moves you towards mastery of your craft.

- It helps manifest your natural voice. This comes about through experience and deconditioning. Deconditioning happens by engaging organically in the writing process and letting things refine as you go. There's no substitute for actual writing time... especially actual writing time that allows for deconstruction, so that you refine your voice rather than simply repeat the same style over and over again.

Who is Freewriting For?

Freewriting is especially beneficial for those who get stuck, who have great ideas but difficulty rendering them in words. In its most basic use-case, freewriting offers a surefire way to get started, a reliable method to engage the flow. In most cases of ordinary stuckness or bogginess, things start to clear up after a few minutes of freewriting.

However, there is more than just one level of getting unstuck. In addition to being blocked about not being able to write at all, there are blocks at deeper levels:

- Your writing doesn't feel true or authentic or good enough.
- Your ideas are jumbled.
- The act of writing feels exhausting.

When you freewrite regularly, you develop the habit of becoming unstuck.

For some reason, we have been trained that stopping to think is the only way to write well. We have not been shown how, actually, continuing to engage the flow can accomplish what we need.

We have been convinced that things should be worked out in the mind before writing. In truth, this just slows everything down.

Freewriting is tremendously effective for clarifying half-formed ideas. You can be playful and tactile with them. By diving in, you can quickly get clear on what research you need to do or what holes there are in your plot that will take work to get right.

Even someone who feels nothing but ease about putting words on the page can benefit from the two-part structure of freewriting, because what some writers really need is an opportunity to hone their inner critic.

It can be a simple discipline: devote the first phase of your writing session to remaining in the creative phase. Write without stopping. Then, devote the second phase to be critical. Revisit your language from a different standpoint, mindful of structure and audience. Hone and refine what works best. Move forward with that and forget about the rest.

Deep freewriting is helpful for writers regardless of what project they want to work on. It is a malleable and flexible writing process. After all, "free" is right there in the title.

Faster than Traditional Thinking

In his book *Accidental Genius*, Mark Levy describes freewriting as "a fast method of thinking onto paper that enables you to reach a level of thinking that's often difficult to attain during the course of a normal business day."

I wholeheartedly agree with him that freewriting attains something that is rarely attained in a normal business day, and in my experience, you can push it further than "thinking on paper."

We need to get beyond the old models of consciousness where thinking is the ever-important achievement. Thinking is great when it's clear. But thinking is far from a complete expression of what is actually happening in our lives.

Remember the models of consciousness from psychology class? No? Well, that's fine too. Picture an iceberg. Maybe one tenth of the iceberg is above the surface. That's the conscious mind, the stuff that we are aware that we are aware of. The part of us that comes on line in the morning after we've had a cup of coffee.

Beneath the surface is 9/10 of the iceberg – the subconscious. The subconscious is us too. That whole thing is us, not just the tip that's above water. The majority of us is down there beneath the water line. I don't know about you, but this makes me curious. What is that part of me doing? What does it like? How can it contribute to my life and the lives of others? If it has 9/10 of my capacity, it seems absurd to ignore this part of me.

And that's not all. Oh, the next part of this is really exciting.

Thus far we have accounted for 10/10ths of the iceberg, but then there's all that stuff surrounding the iceberg. You know, the ocean. That's the unconscious --- the whole ocean. Unbounded, vast, churning. That's us, too, the part of us that is shared. In the churning sea, who is to determine any boundary between self and other?

OK, I hope I have established this concept that we are not merely our thoughts. In fact, we are only barely our thoughts. We are so much more. We are not disembodied brains processing data and moving around perfectly logically.

Freewriting is one way of getting more in touch with the whole self. When we freewrite, we invite more besides the everyday conscious thought-chatter. When freewriting, there will be phases when your feelings, your gut-level knowing, will be more foregrounded than your cerebral activity and something magical or alchemical can happen.

You don't have to believe me. Your experience will show you something like this. Maybe you'd phrase it differently, but my point is. . .

Freewriting can move mountains.

Personal Experience: The 24-Hour Freewriting Marathon

I had the good fortune of attending graduate school alongside Robert David Roe. We were studying creative writing, and when we weren't writing, we were probably either reading or talking about writing. But saddled with coursework and other responsibilities, we both wanted to carve out some extra space to do something really big.

He suggested that we try writing for an extended period of time. It would give us the chance we needed to get deeper into our process and churn out a slew of words. We needed someplace neutral and isolated where we would be undisturbed, where the rest of the world wouldn't exist for us. Some place where we could have what we needed in order to write nonstop for twenty-four hours.

He suggested that we check into a motel, and we did. We brought notebooks, laptops, coffee, and various other charms and talismans to support our grand quest. Dave even brought his own table to work at. We sat at opposite ends of the room, prepared our workspaces, and the rest is history.

I learned a lot about writing by doing this marathon. It goes without saying that I wrote a lot. Without trying very hard, I came up with the drafts for a couple of books of prose poetry, and I did a lot of talking-writing (more on this technique later) to get more clarity about how to navigate all the things I had been learning from my reading and my professors and from my own travels and soul-searching. I wrote my vision for the future and really got inspired by the things that came up. It felt more straightforward and more detailed than I could have imagined. I also came up with several exercises and components that later factored into some intensive retreats I led at retreats around the world.

All this happened for me even though I went into the exercise without having the foggiest notion for a project I wanted to work on. The experience of my first 24-hour freewriting marathon completely changed my life.

I had a big appetite for life-changing experiences, so I looked for another occasion around which I could plan another writing marathon. A couple of months from then, I would have a long boat ride going from one island in the Mediterranean to another. Two nights and one day. I decided to allot the entirety of that middle day to a writing marathon and my focus would be on manifesting my near-term goals. Not just writing goals, but actively manifesting them through writing.

What a perfect use for that time, I thought. In hindsight, I realize that part of what made this second writing marathon so powerful was the way I built it up in my mind. I had absolute certainty that I would go into that session with a single focus and my future depended on it.

Nearly all of the goals that I wrote out for myself came true for me. I vividly imagined them and I wrote about them in present tense. When a limiting belief came up, I used the beauty of flow to attack or undermine or circumnavigate that block or limiting belief. I would not let anything stop me, let alone my own mind or my own beliefs.

One such limiting belief was around how I felt concerned about what my friends would think of me to have taken such a different life and career path from what I thought was normal for someone earning a Master of Fine Arts degree. I was concerned that getting into the self-development space would make me seem weirder to them than I perhaps already did. Embodying wellness and holism and personal transformation went against the grain of that literary culture.

It wasn't just willpower that pushed me forward against my limiting beliefs. It was trust of the process. It was as if the space of the endeavor itself was doing the heavy lifting for me.

Without having to talk myself into things, I was greeted by discoveries and better ways of seeing things. I came to the realization that precisely because I am successful as a retreat facilitator and an author, my friends still think that I am an OK guy. In effect: you can't argue with success. They were my friends, after all. Of course they would want the best for me.

Though many of the limiting beliefs we hold are not very convincing under any real scrutiny, they do nevertheless keep us blocked unless these beliefs get seen for what they are.

My writing marathon brought such tangibility to my beliefs because the feelings, not the thoughts, were at the forefront. The feeling of success was so present with me that nothing else mattered. Lit up by my feelings, I saw things in a truly empowering perspective. It was the fulfillment and the success that I wanted, and I acknowledged that my life would look very different when I got there. Whatever had to change or shift, so be it. I felt big, able to accommodate what needed to be.

I share this experience to give a taste for what is available for you as you embark on this path. There are no limits – by all means, feel free to supersede mine and your own best intentions and wildest ambitions.

Exercise: Set Your Vision for This Journey

The real learning is in doing. And while I share my story with you to give you a sense for what can happen, the options for you are wide open. Your experience is what matters, so it's time for you to get your feet wet.

Try this first freewriting exercise. The guidelines for this first exercise are as follows:

1. Hold in mind a single question.
2. Write without stopping for 10 minutes.

The question: What are my goals? What do I want to unlock by learning deep freewriting?

There is an art to keeping a question in mind during a freewrite. The question doesn't need to be in the forefront of your thinking. You don't want the question to block any idea from coming. Instead, just allow the question to remain there for you in a general sense. Let it be on the backburner, something that you return to periodically.

When you gear your writing into a question like this, it's best not to be rigid or stiff about things. Whatever ideas come, let them be written down. Be fluid and free, while attending to the central concern, which is the question. The question is there for other ideas to gravitate around. It's not that you need to solve the question. You do not need to come up with a final answer that stops you from continuing.

Being curious about the question, what comes up for you? Allow your mind to take departures and get off track, returning to the question and seeing how things evolve as you do so.

Again, there are no right or wrong goals, but just to be sure we are clear, some example goals might be:

- Write a story.
- Write two stories.
- Draft a novel.
- Improve my relationship with writing.
- Uncover my life mission.
- Improve my relationship with life.
- Spread my wings and find my creative voice.
- Try writing in a different style or a different genre.
- Start a journaling habit.
- Keep a daily captain's log.

I share these just to give an idea for general goals that some writers have when they are interested in freewriting.

Having goals brings clarity of outcome. It's not about whether your goal is impressive or sounds good. It's also perfectly all right if part of you feels like your goal might sound silly to someone else. Just go with whatever happens to feel like what you really want.

A solid goal is one that you can feel. Even a clearly-stated goal may not really resonate with you until you have explored the feelings associated with the goal.

Maybe a part of you wants it but other parts of you don't believe you deserve it. That's perfectly normal. Stick with what you really want regardless of anything your inner critic says.

No need to overthink your goal. It's even possible that your goal might shift or change during your process of engaging freewriting around it, almost like it's a living thing.

What constitutes a solid goal is going to be different for each person, and even the same person is likely to be aware of their different goals from moment to moment.

So, look at the clock or set a timer and just dive in to this exercise and see what happens. Keep your pen moving or your fingers typing. No correcting mistakes or looking back at what you've written. If you get stuck, feel free to write nonsense. As you're able, think back to your goal and see what emerges.

Stay with the present moment. Make all the errors you need to. There is no wrong way to do this.

This Isn't Just Another Writing Technique

Now that you have gotten your feet wet and you have your own goal, let's really explore how this method is different from the other methods of writing that you might have already heard about.

In short, deep freewriting strives to take you into the depths of yourself, the parts of the iceberg beneath the water line.

Freewriting is not just some beginner technique to be abandoned when you become a pro. For me personally, it has been the single most impactful practice that I have tried with respect to improving my writing.

Also, this method is alive. It's a flexible method. In the future, it will improve and evolve. If it speaks to you, embrace it and make it yours.

You may have learned about freewriting in school. If so, then it was probably introduced as a way of brainstorming or prewriting, and if you felt how I did about school, then for you, the old way of freewriting sometimes felt like a chore or an obligation, just one other necessary part of the writing process. I don't doubt that you got some good results by following the old method. But we can do better if we adopt the following:

- Every so often, we do nonstop writing marathons. Not only to prove to ourselves that it's possible, but because some of the best stuff can only happen when you're deep into the process. When you only freewrite for a short interval, you're barely getting into the groove. Going for a long duration, you get beneath the surface ideas, the ideas you already know, deeper than the scattered thoughts that anyone could come up with, and into the subconscious, to the ideas that can only come to you once you have cleared out the noise and chatter.
- We adopt an earnest, devotional quality to deep freewriting. No longer are we trying to strip-mine the imagination for whatever idea works for the moment. It's a long term relationship. We're putting in the time because we want to form a healthy and sustainable way of engaging with this mysterious force.
- We are willing to write using any and all mediums. Typing, handwriting, standing up, sitting down, recording the voice. Deep freewriting is about pulling out all the stops, not holding back, making writing an extension of who you are all the time. States of being carry habitual patterns, and when you integrate all sides of you with your desire to write, you tap from those other states. You bring more of your whole self into your endeavor.

- We decide that our end goal is not only to learn a new technique, but to integrate freewriting's underlying philosophy into our everyday writing practice, so that whenever we write, whether we're officially freewriting or not, we reap the rewards of the freewriting we have done in the past. The work we put in now continues to help us years into the future. The progress we make doesn't go away simply because we aren't freewriting. We get to keep the progress that we make.

Improving your writing ability, you clarify your relationship with the flow of ideas from the imagination. Things are not necessarily getting easier for the creative person. It is an increasingly perplexing world out there. Most people are chronically stuck, unable to bring their ideas into physical manifestation. They're stuck behind clouds of bad ideas, many of which are dressed up as good advice. So many people who have the potential of being stellar writers are stuck working lousy jobs, kept busy and exhausted, and stuck watching lousy entertainment. They could be working for themselves. They could be making their own entertainment. They could be clear, going about their daily business with a sense of inspiration and vigor.

Just as today's challenges are more complicated than ever before, the opportunities are also more abundant. Tools are definitely more available, and freewriting is an immensely powerful tool for your self-development arsenal so that you can fully participate in the best the world has to offer.

Deep freewriting belongs to the wave of forward-looking life skills. Never before in the history of civilization have there been so many self-made billionaires or fantastic inventions or leaps in technology. This amazing dissemination of practical information can liberate the well-being of anyone who wants to claim it as their birthright. By stepping out from the confines of the blocked-up mindset, we enter an arena of greater freedom and pure creativity.

Let's Say Our Long Goodbyes to Writer's Block

Writer's block is a general term that I take to mean basically any major hitch in the creative flow. Sure, there are different types of writer's blocks and different durations of it. But to put it most plainly, writer's block is when a writer can't write.

It's a loss of freedom and a loss of identity – a writer who can't write is not really much of a writer. Because of the blow to self-identity that writer's block creates, it's common to invent all sorts of reasons and justifications for being blocked. Plenty of writers spend way more energy fooling themselves that they don't want to write when, really, they just feel blocked. Other writers convince themselves that it's logical since their project is too hard, of course it will be exhausting to write it.

I'm not saying that all writing projects can be manifested in a beeline from start to finish. I understand that different projects have different requirements in terms of their investment of time, energy, research, experience, and collaboration. More often than not, though, writers are working well below their actual capacity.

If you look closely at many of the writers who feel burdened because their project is hard, they're actually not spending their time writing – they're doing other things because they're overwhelmed with their writing and can't bear to face it.

What I'm proposing is that freewriting can effectively address these issues so that writers can achieve their goals and produce whatever written work they really desire to.

Briefly, before getting into the freewriting techniques, I will lay out what underlies many of the blocks that writers often face. We can make our learning a lot more strategic by examining the most common problems that it can solve.

[If, however, you are feeling ready to get your hands dirty with the techniques, you are free at any point to skip on to the Freewriting Agreement exercise.]

Most People Get Blocked Because...

They Set Themselves Up To Be Blocked

What? Yeah, it sounds paradoxical. Who would want to be blocked?

Have you ever had the experience of walking into a room to do something only to end up doing something else entirely? When you entered the room, you had the clear intention to do A, and yet when you got there, you sat down and absentmindedly started doing B. One thing led to another, minutes and hours pass, and the window of time for doing A has gone away completely.

Maybe you have sat down at your computer intending to write, and you end up opening the web browser. You open one tab, another tab, and another. Articles to read, videos to watch, emails to send. Or how about those times when you sit down to write something and instead of writing you sit and stare... at the blank page? out the window? at your shoes?

Let's face it. The write-and-stop method is a way of writing that sets people up to get blocked. When you stop, you drop the flow. Then you sit there, hoping to get hit by another wave of inspiration. When you get an idea, you restart the flow. But sometimes nothing happens.

This block could have been prevented by simply continuing to write. So what if your writing gets off topic? You can delete it later. So what if you don't know what you're saying? When you freewrite, you begin writing before you know what you're going to say. You freely move forward even though the ideas aren't right and the words aren't coherent. It doesn't matter! Incoherence is not the problem. Actually, it's a step in the right direction. Before long, the ideas and the language refines itself, and you are headed towards clarity.

They Expect Their Drafts To Be Good

It takes a measure of humility to be a writer. You have to be patient with yourself and tolerate all sorts of rough spots and potentially embarrassing passages.

When you write a draft, those words and sentences of have been made external and physical thanks to your hard work. And for the moment, it's still just you and that language. No one else is in the picture yet.

Just like any other art form, it's not always glorious to see a written work in progress, and it can be profoundly disorienting for the person working on it.

So even if someone really important is eventually going to read your draft, it's important for you to hold this really clearly in your heart: "Not yet." For the time being, it's still just you and your words. You still have total freedom. Anything can happen.

No worries about how it might appear. It's still being shaped. "Good" or "Bad" don't apply. Drafts are not supposed to be pretty. They're just supposed to exist.

They Expect Their Drafts To Make Sense

Hey, we're creative people, so why shouldn't it be OK for things to be garbled or messy or even profoundly strange from time to time?

If you are working on a sculpture, it's not going to immediately look like what you want it to look like. It takes a lot of time to carve away chunks of material, and it's not ready for criticism until then.

Writing is no different, so let yourself ramble. Tolerate incoherence. Celebrate the tangles and convolutions.

They Mistakenly Believe That Ideas Are Supposed To Occur To Them When They Aren't Writing

Ideas can land at any time. In my experience (and this has been overwhelmingly consistent), ideas tend to land and be the most workable when I am already writing.

With the write-then-stop method, the writer gets an idea and they follow the flow for awhile. Then they drop the flow. Either they get stuck there or they get surprised by an idea, at which point they let themselves write again.

Freewriting is all about starting writing so that airplane after airplane of ideas can pull in for a friendly landing. Your steady flow of words is the runway.

It's as simple as keeping things going. Maintaining forward momentum means you've raised your periscope to behold the domain of ideas. If you don't see anything right away, be patient and just keep scanning the horizons. It's an infinitely abundant place. If you stop and lower your periscope, you're expecting ideas to work pretty hard to find you. They won't always be able to. They might just drift onward and find someone else!

They Have Been Taught That Freewriting Is Just About Venting Or Brainstorming

It's unquestionably valuable for both of these things. I used to think that freewriting was just a way of forcing yourself to blather on so that you could figure out what you wanted to say. I thought freewriting was only about producing throw-away material.

But when I dove into the practice seriously, I saw a couple of significant things about this issue. . .

Firstly, brainstorming doesn't just happen at the beginning phase and then it's over. The more you write, the more you abide with ideas in their raw state, the more they continue to refine and take on a life of their own. The more you immerse yourself in writing without stopping, the more organically this refinement can happen for you.

Secondly, venting your feelings is not of trivial importance. Feelings are your friend, not something to be dismissed or ignored or suppressed. Ideally, you want your writing to be informed and vitalized by your actual feelings. Feelings have so much more to offer than mere thoughts. What could be more valuable than your depth of feeling?

When you're writing, if you ignore or suppress how you are really feeling about your life or about a character or scene, that is going to get in the way of the quality of scene that you write.

My suggestion is to try it. The next time you write, experiment with this. See the difference you can make by simply acknowledging what you are actually feeling as you work on whatever it is you are working on. Acknowledging what you are actually feeling can pivot you towards an insight that otherwise would remain locked away.

Be bold and turn towards your uncomfortable emotions. Face them, and when they are present, write about them.

Debunking Misconceptions About Freewriting

People don't take to the streets with banners and signs protesting freewriting. The problem isn't that freewriting is castigated. The problem is that freewriting is overlooked. Worse, people undersell freewriting. They have only been shown a small fraction of what this powerful practice is capable of. They think that the correct way to write is to get blocked up and wait for inspiration to find a way in.

There are plenty of common misconceptions that I will do my best to clarify here. I do this because these beliefs and ideas basically blow around in the environment, and, like a common virus, it's likely that you yourself may have contracted one or another at some point.

It's important to bring awareness to these arguments or beliefs and see whether you really believe them to be true. We all go around every day carrying all sorts of unexamined beliefs that limit us. If would only bring these beliefs into awareness, we would gain some freedom to decide whether we want to live in line with them or not.

A belief that isn't truly yours is something you can let go of, and you'll be a lot more free because of it. The beliefs listed below are all misconceptions that I have had or have heard someone else share.

"The purpose of freewriting is to fill as much space with as much language as fast as possible."

Freewriting guarantees quantity, but it's not ideal to limit ourselves to believe that is what it's best at.

Freewriting is about being in the flow. Whether this means working at a all-out run or a steady plod forward, the main thing is that there is a flow and that you're in it. It can produce a lot of words, but that's not what really matters. Ultimately, most writers want their efforts at writing to produce something good.

We get better at what we practice, and if we practice writing and pausing, then we build a resistance to doing things any other way, even if there is a more direct and fulfilling way. We start to believe it isn't even possible to have a direct way towards prolific writing.

The process of freewriting does not merely generate a lot of words on many pages. It's also a practice for skillfully navigating your thoughts and feelings so that the abundance of words you fill the pages with is an abundance you are happy with.

"When I read back through my freewriting, I don't like the way I sound."

Voice evolves over time. We write in imitation of those we admire. We react to criticism we have had in the past, or that we have put on ourselves for one reason or another.

A writer's voice is in some measure forged intentionally, but a great deal also happens automatically, simply by engaging the process. Much about a writer's voice stems from habits and deep down aspects that are core to your personality.

When we try to sound a different way in our writing, we're either dressing up our natural voice in some way (trying for ornate or eloquent) or we're stripping away the nonessentials and paring down (for simplicity or directness).

When writing, we tap from different sides of ourselves at different times. It's fair to look at these sides as characters or sub-personalities within us. It's not uncommon for me to draw from my professor persona when writing something nonfiction and instructional. When I write an email to a friend, I generally draw from my inner goof. It's not so much in what I say but how I say it.

If the voice fits the project, it usually works fine. But as with anything else, the longer you spend time with it, the more you can grow sensitive to it. Think of taking a road trip with your tennis buddy. Maybe you get along fine with them when you're on the court, but spend eight hours next to them in the car and you see a whole other side of them. You grow keenly aware of their annoying mannerisms.

When looking back through a freewriting session, you might not like everything you see, and maybe it has nothing to do with the ideas or words, but something about yourself that you're not resolved about. Don't let this stop you.

Cut and paste is a beautiful thing. Of course, you can delete the obvious rubbish, but you also have the opportunity to extract whatever material that you choose, perhaps put it in a different document altogether, and otherwise learn from the experience of cleaning up and unifying multiple projects.

As you read and skim what you have written, tune in to the qualities of your voice and ask questions rather than judge.

Look closer at what you don't like. What kind of character does it portray to you? Does it remind you of someone? What do you like about it? What might you be able to like?

Like it or not, our experiences do shape our voice. But there is nothing to be gained by negatively judging these parts of us or trying to hide them. We should work with what we've got. With my professorial voice, there are definitely times when I read back through something and I dislike that it sounds tight-assed and authoritarian. I ask myself what it is missing, and often I conclude that I am not really feeling much of my own presence and warmth there. By adding a few stories and examples and revisiting some of my wording, the problem has been solved.

Freewriting is all about honoring what's working. When I allow judgment to make my decisions, I miss out on workable material and my projects grind to a halt. It isn't bad or wrong that I have an inner professor. It's OK that the way things first came out needed a bit of restructuring. When things are regarded as being "in process," we keep the opportunity to add missing elements and reshape things so that they ring true.

"I shouldn't keep writing when I don't know what I'm going to say next."

When you hear yourself or someone else say this, turn the statement upside-down. What happens when you give yourself permission to write even when you feel unsure of the right words?

You can pivot the belief that writing should only come once you have everything figured out by finding the courage to embrace uncertainty. It's simple to begin such a pivot, but it's not always going to feel easy. I don't want to underplay this. It takes courage to freewrite.

When you feel really blocked, the experience can be as awful as standing in front of a room of people when they're all expecting you to give a speech and you have no idea what to say. You don't have anything prepared and you are laden by the weight of each millisecond as they expect to hear something from you, and it had better be impressive.

If you notice that you feel this way, you have the opportunity to flip the belief around. You can reposition your relationship to it and get in touch with the part of you that equates uncertainty with adventure. You can coax the courage out of yourself by making small shifts of mind to engage your natural inborn curiosity, to trust yourself. The curiosity is there. Instead of taking things personally, step out of the way and ask questions that can invite positive solutions. Don't let this belief be an excuse that prevents you from writing. Try the talking-writing technique and shake loose from the fear and reawaken your innate sense of vivacious curiosity.

If you want an outline, you can freewrite one! When you feel like your writing isn't going anywhere, you can ask questions to help yourself find out where to take things. Where do you want it to go? What is missing? As you write, you can ask questions that direct your focus right to where you need to make the improvements.

It's totally fine that your writing isn't perfect yet, or that it isn't shaped the way it needs to be. It's a work in progress. It's not wrong that you're criticizing yourself, but it's unproductive to draw negative conclusions from your criticism. Why not use that criticism to sharpen your vision so that you can hunt for what's missing? As you're doing that, you can avoid your critical voice from veering into negativity by reminding yourself of what you want it to feel like. Does the piece feel alive? What feels best about it? What would your reader want to see more of? What is the expected structure based on the sort of project you're working on?

If you know your reader's expectations based on what kind of project it is, you have an entry point for who to speak to and how to speak to them. Give your audience what they want, and in turn, they want to see you enjoy yourself in your writing.

Becoming a freewriter doesn't mean abandoning your study of organizational methods and story structure. There's everything to be gained by familiarizing yourself with the kind of structure that readers expect. Just don't lose your sense of enjoyment when doing so. Too many writers get hijacked by their inner critic who values too highly the notion of "correct" story structure.

Most people have their preferred writing setup. For some, it's a quiet desk in a private office. For others, it's a corner table in a boisterous coffee shop.

I used to be inseparable from my handwritten journal. I carried one everywhere I went. I have amassed stacks of filled journals. I traveled the world, and no matter where I was, whether beachside or in the middle of a crowded city, I had my journal strapped to my shoulder. I would write whenever I had something to say.

In retrospect, I also notice that there had been plenty of opportune times to write that I missed out on not because I didn't have anything to work on but because I thought I didn't feel like it. Looking back now, I realize that these missed opportunities were more the fault of a belief that I didn't have anything good to say than that I didn't feel like writing. Deep down, I wanted to write whenever and wherever. Big picture, I had projects that I could have been working on. But in the moment, I got caught in the negative belief that I didn't feel like it. I was afraid of writing garbage, so I held back. I only let myself write when I felt positively enthused about some idea.

Experience has taught me that only writing when in a certain state isn't really the best because the writer becomes handicapped to a given situation. We all have our ideal scenarios to write, but we should be able to write pretty much wherever and whenever.

The main thing is that feeling like it (or not) is not actually any guarantee of whether we will write good material during the writing session. Maybe you have heard about the trick people use to get themselves to go for a run. They don't feel like running, but they know they should, so they say, "Well, I'll just go for five minutes." Five minutes sounds easy, so they follow through. And the majority of the time, that five minutes turns into thirty or however long they really know they needed to. The same holds true for writing. So much can happen if you can just ease yourself over the threshold into doing it.

With regard to my relationship with writing, I now understand that there are energetic highs and lows. Only choosing the highs and bailing out on the lows wasn't helping me improve as a writer. It very often happens that the best writing sessions happen when I'm in a bit of a funk but I lightly push through it. Pushing through it is an act of trust and will, and there are good discoveries to be made on the other side of the initial darkness. Just because you don't feel like it (or you don't think that you feel like it) doesn't mean you'll write garbage. The opposite could even be true sometimes.

Everybody writes stuff that won't see the light of day. That doesn't mean it should get judged negatively. I now see this material as part of the process rather than a failure. Adopting a healthy attitude with regard to writing complete crap is crucial for your productivity, your longevity as a writer and for overall self-acceptance.

Freewriting is about being witness to the flow of ideas. Being creative means not placing limits on what you're aware of as you're doing it. If you write useless stuff, that's fine in the same way that writing a masterpiece is fine.

You're not being made to show anyone else your writing if it turns out to be a pile of shit, so there is no need to be unduly afraid of the possibility of writing poorly. By adopting the practice of freewriting, you are being invited to freewrite, plain and simple. So even when you don't think you feel like it, if that quiet voice within you suspects that you do maybe want to write, then don't let anything stand in your way.

"I don't like to write fast."

It's fine to have preferences. All writers like to write at different speeds at different times. Some writers love when they are propelled by an intense urgency that compels them to write as fast as possible. This can be particularly true for visual thinkers.

Other writers, often of a more kinesthetic orientation, like to feel their language and write at a slow and steady rhythm. Some projects need to be written quickly. Others would become a disaster if the writer insisted on insensitively speeding through things.

Freewriting gets you to continue moving forward at a steady pace. At times, you will resist it. At other times, it will feel natural, transparent, and you won't even realize that you are holding yourself to the steady forward pace because the imagination's rhythm will carry you forward with a sense of momentum.

Freewriting gets you to write outside the habitual start-stop pacing. It's good to change things up because the force behind the shift involves moving into greater alliance with flow.

Practice with steady forward momentum can cascade into other positive shifts. When you overcome one resistance, you allow the momentum of acceptance and equanimity to bring about greater self-discovery.

"I need to know where I'm going."

It's understandable for writers to get frustrated about not knowing where to go. If you don't know what you should say what point is there in trying to say something?

The peculiar thing is that even when you don't know what you want to say, you're still that peculiar breed of human who believes they do have things to say. It may be subtle and it may be loud, but the need, the craving, it's there.

Your deep and subtle desire to put things into words may not be accessible if you merely permit yourself to think about writing, or if you are gripped by the need to get things right. But if you give yourself permission to feel your writing, magic happens.

It's OK to not know where you're going sometimes. Just notice how you feel when this belief arises and continue moving forward. Use freewriting to help you figure out where you want to go.

The more awareness you have of how you feel, the more you notice where the negative belief is coming from. With a bit of skill and some introspection, you can use deep freewriting strategies to more efficiently find what you want to say. You can use freewriting to talk things out with yourself, map out possibilities, explore scenarios, even jot possible structures you could use. Even if it is vague or rough or all out of order, the simple act of continuing forward momentum will quickly bring you much better results than if you had stopped.

"I know what I want to say, so there's no use freewriting."

Freewriting is useful for when you want to brainstorm ideas, and the technique becomes much deeper the more you engage it. It brings about a change in relationship between you and the imagination. By consistently showing up for the steady stream of creative flow, you become more of the writer you were born to be.

When you follow through with your desire to freewrite whether or not you have a clear notion of what to say, you send a signal that you are still open to receive inspiration.

Even with a very detailed outline, there are going to be opportunities to be astounded by something original. And if that was not the case, if you choose to freewrite even when you are already clear about your direction, then you will likely arrive at that destination much sooner than with any other style of writing.

Reprogramming Your Inner Writer: The Freewriting Agreement

It's time to delete the old programming, to overthrow the tyranny of writer's block. Limiting beliefs hold hostage the creative impulse, hijack your best ideas, and insist that things need to be perfect or else you shouldn't write.

So what do we do? Let's make an agreement with ourselves. An agreement between the creative impulse and the critical impulse. Under the old rules, the critical voice blocked us, not because it was bad, but because it wasn't fully seen and recognized.

We acknowledge that the inner critic has something it wants to offer us. It wants our writing to conform to its model of what is good, beautiful, and true.

Well, we can make a win-win agreement. Both the critical impulse and the creative impulse can be celebrated.

One option for crafting a freewriting agreement is, of course, to freewrite it. After you finish reading this section, take the next ten minutes to jot out the various inner elements of freewriting you would like to hold yourself accountable to.

If you'd like, you can draft out a written agreement you can sign and date, something like this:

I hereby agree to embrace the new practice of freewriting.

- *When I choose to, I will write without stopping for a given duration.*
- *I will remain present with my writing.*
- *I will resist making edits or looking back at what I wrote.*
- *I won't criticize or judge while I write.*
- *I will stay in the creative mode until I am finished.*
- *I look forward to having the option of coming back later if I want to improve things.*

Signed,

_________________ *'s creative and critical impulses*

Under this new agreement both sides win. The creative wins because it gets to lead the way. The critical wins because it gets the final say.

Your inner critic agrees to wait until the creative has spoken. First comes the creative. You write and let it flow, totally free. In your freedom, you are bound to make a mess of things.

Any mess is a delicious opportunity for your critic. Unpolished writing begs for its care and attention, as a machine full of misplaced and broken parts begs for the mechanic to make repairs and get it to purr.

The creative gets to have all the space it wants, and the critic is assured there will be something to work on, some overripe disaster awaiting cleanup. The creative's role is to burst with joy from the pages. Later, the critic can geek out on revising. Remember how strong the pull is to correct your wording as you freewrite, to add a comma or fix a spelling error? Well, under the new agreement, there will be no more fighting for bits and scraps! There will be pages upon pages of rough material just waiting for the critic's expert eye.

It's not so different from the practice held by many traditional cultures or sharing circles where the person whose turn is to speak holds the staff or peace flower. When it's that person's turn to speak, it's everyone else's turn to listen. Freewriting is about honoring this kind of agreement.

It takes a bit of discipline, so you make an agreement and give yourself space. This agreement gives you something that you can rest on. In time, it will come to feel like an armchair made just for you, a driver's seat with everything you need in the right place.

I feel the need to emphasize here and elsewhere that the critical is not bad. The critical impulse gets the short end of the stick because it has been encouraged to come up when it isn't welcome. Really, this is the fault of how we get taught to write. We get penalized for mistakes, so out of fear and distrust, we keep the critical impulse near at hand as we write.

My challenge to you is to make your own freewriting agreement.

It's time to throw off the conditioning and declare your independence. From this point forward, you can do things differently. There is no need to worry as you write whether your writing is OK. Freewriting is about learning to rest on your own authority, and that means embracing vulnerability and uncertainty.

People get a temporary shot of certainty when they declare that something is right or it's wrong. When something is new, we can't always be so certain. Nobody can tell us just yet. When it's still being formed, it's neither good nor bad, right nor wrong.

Part of what it means to be an author is to be able to rest on that kind of authority. It's not credentials, not how many books or fans, it's how you rest in your own relationship with the imagination.

No tricks, nothing fancy, just you and your words.

Authority Exercise

Take a few minutes to freewrite about the things you love most about writing and any of the things you have learned that you would like to let go of. This sounds really simple, but the effects can be dramatic.

During the summer after I graduated with my MFA degree in Creative Writing, I spent hours each morning doing this writing exercise. Then I did deep breathing, went for a long run, and came back and did this exercise even more. I wanted to reposition myself for the future, to embrace what I loved most deeply about writing and to let go of the things I had been taught that I did not personally believe.

I repeated the exercise each day, and even, no doubt, ended up repeating myself in my writing many times. The importance was on feeling the states behind the writing rather than the words I wrote. I credit this practice with recentering me and getting me more in touch with my authentic depth.

Daily Practice: Morning Freewrite

As part of your decision to embrace freewriting, I highly recommend adopting this daily practice for at least a few weeks.

The exercise is to do a brief freewrite as soon as possible after waking. Ideally, make this so brief that it doesn't interfere in any way with your current schedule. Shoot for two or three pages each morning. Nothing too much. Just enough to engage the flow of the written word upon waking. Just write for a couple of minutes or a couple of pages, close your notebook and move on.

The first moments after waking are an opportune time to write your dreams, if you remember them. The more regularly you hold this practice, the easier you may find it to recall your dreams.

Write how you're feeling, any ideas you have, the things you're worried about, or whatever is present to you. Let it be inarticulate and completely thoughtless. It's not about planning your day. To leap too far into planning your day would be to skip what this practice is all about.

It's a mind dump. We accrue all sorts of stuff while we sleep that is ready to be released upon waking. Why wake and take a shower to wash your body, yet go around carrying the stuff in your mind left over from the night before? I feel far fresher when I do a morning freewrite.

When you sleep, the body enters a state of restorative chaos. Energy reconfigures and you are able to dream, heal and process things. When you wake, you click back into the conscious mind and your waking sense of self, but right there in those first moments is a groggy window of time where things don't instantly click.

The day's first moments bring an opportune window to do practices that cleanse and clear and awaken our energy, things like showering, breathing exercises, gentle stretches, and a short morning freewrite.

The aim here is to clear the mind by releasing whatever happens to be there at the moment. This helps process things, and it works best when you don't try very hard. As much as possible, you should give yourself over to the simplicity of the practice and observe the results.

When I do a morning freewrite, I notice that I feel more energetic and fresh throughout the day. Not because of anything physiological, but because my mind is less cloudy and my emotions are somewhat more accessible and clear.

I tend to think of it kind of like doing neti for the writer's mind. Just as neti rinses the sinuses and awakens clarity of breath, your morning freewrite rinses and awakens the mind by getting rid of old stuff, just bits and pieces of ideas and concerns.

It's about releasing things so you can more fully engage the flow of the present. An added benefit of doing this practice is that the writing you do later in the day will come easier for you.

Again, I want to emphasize that your job is not to shape anything or plan anything. Doing so would leap too far into the normal waking state. Far better to engage the writing process while allowing yourself to stay fuzzy and even incoherent, contradictory or meandering.

Not only is it a practice in self-acceptance, it also brings a sense of gentleness and stillness to the less conscious parts of you that actually have a lot to offer in the way of creativity.

To recap, the idea of the morning freewrite is to let go of what you have in your mind. The aim is definitely not to write something that needs to accomplish anything. Quite the opposite. Simply write what is there to give it a home outside of you, sort of the way the wizards in Harry Potter take their wands and pull out memories to use in the pensieve. You write it to be free of it. That in itself creates a subtle momentum which can have a powerful effect on the way you write and how you feel for the rest of the day.

Module I Recap

- Every morning, freewrite in your morning journal for at least a couple of pages. Dump it all out onto the page.

- Repeat the authority exercise a few times to get recentered with what you love about writing.
- Continue to refine your goals and vision.

Module 2: Structured Freewriting

An Invigorating Way to Think About Structure and Organization

While there is nothing wrong with using freewriting techniques to brainstorm a few quick and dirty ideas, it is also true that you can use freewriting to produce clear and well ordered drafts. Two techniques that are especially useful with this are the sketch and bird's eye mode.

These techniques are versatile and adaptable so that no matter your preference or style, you will be able to make use of them in a way that feels natural and intuitive. Essentially, this means they won't come to feel like techniques at all, but rather an extension of your own intent. With practice, your writing can more readily come out how you would want it to look in the end.

It's ironic, because the freewriting journey brings you towards an outcome of greater efficiency precisely by relinquishing the obsession about getting things right.

Trying to write and edit at the same time will never get you there. It's like stop-and-go driving. It sucks, it wears down your car, and by the time you get to your destination, you're stressed and exhausted. Freewriting is more like how they allow motorcycles (in California, anyway) to ride in between the lanes of traffic, thereby not having to stop despite traffic jams.

Freewriting improves your internalized know-how of how to structure your writing, organize your thoughts on the fly, and write things in a way that feels organic.

One of the best ways to get better at something is to practice it a lot, and when you freewrite, you spend all your time in the flow of creation. There's much more voltage in the creative spume than at the editing desk. The increased voltage of the practice can give the freewriter the experience not only of being in the flow but also of having better perspective, higher elevation with respect to their writing project.

Because a freewriter is immersed in their process, they are better able to feel how it feels from the inside out. The more we live inside a project, the better able we can become at organizing and summarizing it.

A typical way to think about structure with regard to writing is to look at the desired end product.

Say you're writing a nonfiction book on how to find a reliable used car. There is more than one right way of structuring your writing; you have a lot of freedom with how to order information in that book. You could begin with a story based on your own experience, something that draws your reader in and gets them to connect with you as a person. You could also start in a very technical manner, having them break down their quest for an ideal car according to their budget and what suits their lifestyle. The main thing to keep in mind is that your ideas about the end result definitely do not need to be locked in and fully predetermined, so that you must absolutely write the book in a very specific order, with no departures from your overall plan.

In a practical sense, each individual project must find its own organization determined by the logic that underlies its various parts. By logic, I mean that there is a reason why one part should follow another part.

The order of writing in the book does not always need to be mirrored by the order in which you write it. You should write things in the order they are presented to you. No need to put off the ideas that are actually coming to you right now. You can either reorder the material later or you can experiment with making the existing order work.

When in doubt, just don't overthink it. Imagine instead that you are drawing a diagram for someone on a cocktail napkin, using arrows to indicate major shifts in organization. If it works, it works, right?

How you order things is all about the expectations of your reader and what feels right for the specific project you're working on. Don't reorder things just because it seems correct to do so. Go with what feels the most alive.

A project's underlying logic can find expression in a variety of ways, and when you look at things from a bare-bones perspective, you can better embrace the freedom to generate things in the right order. Focusing on structure as if it were an obligation, something arbitrarily imposed, will not help the flow of ideas.

You don't have to wait to write something because you think it belongs at the end. You are free to generate material in any order. If you write something first that you know really has to go near the end of the book, that's great too, because you already know where to put it. Write a note to yourself during your freewrite to remind yourself of this need to reorder and then keep flowing.

Wildness and Messiness

Here, I'm defining two different terms with respect to how they describe freewriting: wildness and messiness. The short answer is that wildness is preferable and messiness can be tough to work with. The more you freewrite, the more you will get a sense for determining whether a given chunk of writing is either messy or wild (or both or neither).

Wildness

Writing that is wild might not be polished or perfectly ordered, but it nevertheless shines with possibility. With wild writing, there is the sense of being helped, that the piece itself wants to be written. In wildness is richness, depth, and vitality. Wild writing is both confident and malleable. When rereading wild writing, your inner critic feels enlivened, guided by the sparks of your creative impulse.

Messiness

Writing I label messy feels boggy, convoluted, heavy yet lacking substance. It reads like the author is attached to their own wording yet they don't know what they're driving towards. It's as if something in the sentences wraps back around on themselves and hooks the writer's ideas, preventing them from taking flight.

One antidote to messiness is being able to discern different stages of the process. How is this possible? Having a good workflow helps. This means focusing on one element of your writing project at a time. This doesn't mean you need to know everything in advance. It only means that you decide to channel all your creativity towards a single specific aim at a time.

You remember the importance of separating the creative versus the critical impulse so that you don't try to write and revise at the same time? This advice is similar. If you're struggling with messy writing, it is likely that you are trying to look in too many directions at once.

Example Workflow

Let's say you're writing a fantasy novel. You are structuring your workflow so that you only tackle one main element at time. First, you decide that you're going to focus all your creative force on exploring your world.

In this phase, you want to learn about your characters, the different settings and plot dynamics, the scenes you want to have. This phase is about discovering more about what you want to write. So, the writing that you do all flows into that bucket.

This writing can be all over the place, because your expectations are clear. What you write isn't a draft, it's an exploration of the world. It doesn't matter what happens with the material you write. You can extract some bits or just leave it all as part of the process.

When you feel done with that phase, you move forward with the next step of your workflow, which is to begin experimenting with the order you want to tell your story in. You write and write about different ideas and describe how you picture it all story-boarded.

After that, you channel your creativity to generate some material and keep going until you have a huge amazing draft. You have a sense for where everything belongs because you already explored the world and produced a kind of storyboard for yourself – nothing official, just in a way that worked for you.

Because you are held by a clear impulse with each phase of writing, you have avoided messy writing. Perhaps at times your writing became chaotic or all over the place, but it was nevertheless contained within the general brackets of your driving intent.

It's really important that you not try to work on the whole project at the same time. It pays dividends when you have a writing process that supports your ability to know what you know, and know what you don't know. By gearing your creative impulse into one major goal at a time, you only need to do a little bit to make a major step forward. You save a lot of time and energy. Instead of having a mess on your hands, you have wildness that is efficient. It's the best of both worlds.

Even the wildest of things can fit together if you have a really good workflow. A good workflow is a fluid and adaptable process that can work in a variety of scenarios or types of writing projects. At its most simple implementation, a workflow can be as basic as having the intention to work on only one aspect of writing at a time.

With that said, let's move on to an exercise that you can begin to use immediately in your writing workflow.

Sketching Exercise

The sketching technique revolutionized my efficiency as a writer.

With a sketch, you have a glimpse of the whole project in miniature. When you have a sketch to work from, it is easy to keep the entirety of your freewriting relevant to your main topic or idea.

The sketching technique builds on the same logic behind basic freewriting, that you're most effective when you focus all your energy on doing a single thing at a time. In the case of a sketch, you get to engage your inner critic right at the beginning of a writing session. You use it to create a map for yourself of your terrain.

I find that I can write with a greater sense of ease when I know where every element stands in proportion to each other. When your plan is an organic one, arrived at on the spot, then it is alive and spontaneous and you can use it to structure your thinking so that you stay in that nice forward momentum while also remaining relevant with your main topic.

So what is a sketch? Essentially, it's a step in the workflow dedicated to looking at the main ideas. After completing the sketch, then you freewrite in earnest.

The idea behind sketching is as simple as it sounds. A sketch is a jotty bit of writing where you just put down the main ideas. They don't have to be the perfect ideas or the final chapter titles or anything official. It's all about what works for you based on how you like to work. This method is analogous to the technique used by many painters. To start a painting, the painter may first use pencil or charcoal or a light color of paint and quickly put down some of the primary elements of what they're painting, only later going in and covering up the sketch with the actual painting.

The sketch is helpful to get the main structural elements right and to be sure what fits where. When you start with a sketch, you invite a bit of the critical impulse to help plan where you can later go by flowing with the creative impulse.

Let's look at a couple of different ways of implementing the sketching technique.

Outline Sketch

With this style of outlining, you do a quick initial freewrite to draft your sketch. Then you use that sketch like an outline to organize a second, longer freewrite.

Freewrite to make an initial sketch of your project. In your freewriting, try to develop phrases or sentences stating what wants to happen, in order. Continue until you're done.

This is a mode of freewriting, so when you make a sketch, you want to abide by the guidelines of freewriting. Don't stop and think – just keep writing. As you write, you can allow yourself to get off track or go incoherent. Just keep feeling forward towards where you want the piece to go. You don't need to have a ton of detail. When you read back through your sketch, all you're looking for are the bits and highlights, little nuggets and elements from which to later build your piece. And if they're out of order, that's OK too. Just leave a clue for yourself in the freewrite itself so the correct order is going to be clear to you when you read back through.

Once you have a rough outline of your project, begin another freewriting session to fill in each section of the outline.

Example:

> Sandra has dinner with Milford, and his mom arrives halfway through. blah blah blah Milford accidentally lets slip some clue about his dark past. tangent about the current political situation in Iceland and how it reminds you of a Greek myth you misheard at a party years back. Sandra departs with his mother, leaving Milford alone, staring into his clam chowder.

Leave spaces in between the sentences and fill in the details. Think of the sketched material almost like headers for the material that goes there. Maybe you need a paragraph or maybe you need several pages. It all depends on how high-elevation your sketch was.

Example:

> Sandra has dinner with Milford.
> His mom arrives halfway through.
> Milford accidentally lets slip some clue about his dark past.
> Sandra departs with his mother, leaving Milford alone, staring into his clam chowder.

Tip: don't leave any gaps, and by this I mean don't skip over any sections if you can help it. Even if you don't know what to put there, try and put at least something there rather than leaving a puzzle for yourself later. Sometimes the really dumb ideas actually work out fine, and when you have something there, you have something to improve upon. Just keep going with the freewrite fleshing out your outline in order.

If as you write you notice that a part feels dull, then maybe it is dull, and you don't need it. It's almost certain you can address that material in some other way so that it doesn't feel obligatory. If it's dull for you, it will probably bore your reader. Seldom is enough correct information really what holds a story back.

If you acknowledge that it's dull but you really do need it to be there, do something to make it interesting. Barring that, try making it pass quickly. Maybe instead of showing the whole scene, you can simply pass that material to the reader as a voiceover or expository language in one swift stroke and be done with it. Even though the common wisdom is "show, don't tell," if the alternative is showing a boring scene, then telling could be preferable, depending on your style. Instead of showing a long drawn-out dinner scene, you can say what was boring about the dinner scene, according to your point of view character, and have that judgment pass some insight to the reader.

Benefits of This Technique

The sketching technique is a very light and easy way of making your writing time efficient and on point. It eliminates down-time, thinking time, and getting off track. You know where you need to go because you lightly charted the path. It's penciled in. Sketching prepares you for the experience of later embodying, traversing, and living inside what you see glimpses of.

It's hard to go wrong with sketching, provided that you do it in such a way that harmonizes with the lived-in space of the book. What this means: Don't force yourself to follow some outwardly imposed idea for a correct scene outline. Simply notate what stands out to you. A good sketch is all about making things workable for you. What feels right for the story? What will give you and your reader joy?

Sketching can lead to some ongoing major breakthrough in productivity. The author Rachel Aaron describes a similar technique in her book *2k to 10k*. She credits doing a preliminary sketch with a huge performance leap in her daily writing process.

Are There Any Drawbacks?

For me, there are not many cons to the sketch technique. This is my preferred way to write most projects, and it's the way I begin many writing sessions.

It does require that you do some organizational work early in the process, and for some people that's not appealing. They believe that when they jot out an outline it will kill their sense of discovery.

For me, all I can say is that I actually notice more sense of discovery with this method than with any other, because I discover the outline itself through freewriting and I continue my discovery-making as I fill in the outline with material. Plus, it pays dividends in productivity. Once I have a good outline, there is no time wasted deliberating on what part needs to go where.

Because I continue to make discoveries each step along the way, it sometimes happens that I still need to reorder my material later in the draft. A sketch is not always able to account for the way things will emerge, but that's not the fault of the sketch. Discovery is inherent in the process, and readjustments are often going to be necessary.

Reordering can be frustrating, but never as frustrating as when writing with no outline or sense of structure at all. Reordering is much easier to do when at the sketching phase of things.

Wash-Away Sketch: Jot It, Then Let Go

The technique:

- Make an initial sketch simply to explore the flow
- Read back through the sketch to note the general structure
- Leave the sketch behind
- Freewrite

This method is ideal for using the first phase of freewriting to get the juices flowing, and it's a really nice practice to be able to hold that high-elevation sense of organization in the back of the mind rather than right there on the page.

Sometimes when the outline is there on the page it can feel obligatory, and it's a challenge to give one element its due because the writer has a compulsion for moving on to the next one. In those cases, the ideal approach is a sketch that you wash away once you're finished with it. It's a great practice for being able to internalize your outline and then to let it all go if during the actual writing session things need to shift around, whether a little or a lot.

What This Looks Like

Let's say you want to write for an hour on the next chapter in your novel. This is the first draft of the book and you want to discover it as you go. You don't have an outline or storyboards. So you get yourself a cup of tea, sit down at your desk, and...

- Devote five minutes to freewriting about the glimpses and impressions you get about the chapter you want to write. As you freewrite, make note of any sections that stand out.
- Take a minute to go back through your writing and delete everything except for the highlights.

- Put the highlights in the order you'd like them to occur.
- Freewrite for the remaining ten minutes or so to develop a workable sketch of the significant moments or elements in this chapter.
- Read back through your highlights and second freewrite, noting the main movements and their order.
- Delete or set aside this writing and begin to draft your chapter.

Pros of This Method

It's a way of gearing into things and then moving it out of the way. This is good if you really need things to be organic and you are more in a discovery phase. Or, if you totally trust your understanding of the material such that once you remind yourself of what you want to cover, you can do it. The writing will flow as a seamless whole, without having the speed bumps or joints between the outlined nodes.

Cons of This Method

As with anytime you delete something, you might accidentally get rid of something you wanted to keep. Memory isn't perfect, and neither are attention spans. Sometimes the flow that is happening in the moment is different from the flow you want to record. Maybe you were more at the heart of the matter when you did the initial sketch and then you veered gradually off-track. It's possible, but worth risking. The more likely thing to happen is that you will misremember the sketch but what ends up emerging has a more seamless and organic feel than writing that had been stitched artificially together so that it fits an outline.

The Gradual Sketch

This technique is about moving gradually from the initial idea towards a full draft. Whereas in previous techniques the sketch is something you produce all in one go, with a gradual sketch, you can keep coming back to the sketch phase of a project until it feels ready to move forward with. You can take five minutes one day and another five minutes a month later, or you can do it all in a single writing session.

To begin, all you need is a vague or general notion of what you want to write.

Here is one way the gradual sketch might look:

- Sketch for five minutes and then read back through what you have. This is just a brief partial sketch, not a full sketch. Leave gaps and missing parts. Do this first sketch just to move from pregnant chaos into form.
- Later, whether minutes or months, add to that sketch. Make a second solid pass through, adding material and rounding things out a bit. Feel free to retain placeholders in the sections where you know there should be something but for which you're drawing a blank.
- Repeat until you feel complete.

With the gradual sketch technique, you're invited to focus on only what interests you at the moment, to write about what feels alive to you about your project right now.

You are free to make a sketch of the entire project if what feels alive to you is all over the place. To do it right, the gradual sketch does not need to develop anything right away, whether broad in scope or narrow, into an outline. It only needs to take you to where you have something a bit more concrete to work with.

Maybe you want to do a gradual sketch on a scene or a resonant section of your project. It might be a few aspects of the whole project that you want to think about or retool.

However you want to use it, the exercise gives you the opportunity to feel through the terrain of your project and explore their order, relationship and significance. It gives you an opportunity to test the waters, prod and poke your idea, experiment with your hypothesis, feel things out, and move leisurely towards greater mastery of your content.

Module 2 Recap

- Morning journal
- Try out each kind of sketch with a freewriting session of at least 10 minutes each

Module 3: The Power of Time and Questions

Thus far, you have delved into a new way to freewrite and are beginning to get your hands dirty. You have adopted a regular morning freewriting practice.

How are you doing with your goals for this course? How is the sketching technique working for you? The sketching technique is one that will stay with us as we move forward. It's a keeper, for sure.

Though freewriting is definitely a practice that gets you into more of a wild, natural, flexible mindset, generally writers prefer to produce material that isn't totally all over the place, purely messy. We want to easily be able to make use of our freewritten stuff.

With that in mind, in this module the focus is on giving you some more formulas to help make your freewriting sessions even less boggy, less tangled, less messy, and more clear, more on track.

Despite how loathsome messy drafts can be, you need to let yourself go there. Paradoxically, it's necessary to embrace chaos, uncertainty, and the fear of total incoherence. When you're freewriting and you notice that you are becoming resistant to uncertainty, stay with it. Let yourself feel the fear of the bog and nevertheless continue to trust the process.

Each step forward is one step closer to mastery. Be patient with yourself and with the wild flows of imagination and inspiration. The more you stick with it, the more freewriting reveals itself as a direct path for becoming a more efficient, unburdened, and transparent writer.

It is a living and evolving practice. Let's explore a couple of different techniques that tweak your freewriting.

Hot Seat Mode

This type of freewriting I call Hot Seat Mode. It's a great way to begin a writing session to blow out the cobwebs. Use it to steamroll and stumble through whatever language the imagination makes available to you.

The objective is to step into greater confidence and to decouple the feeling of confidence from the need to prove it externally. You don't need to be good at something to have confidence in yourself. And when you have confidence, you are more likely to do a good job at whatever you're doing.

Prior to this exercise, you will need to gather a series of questions that guide you towards a resolution. An example of this type of question would be "My gut sense for this character is. . ." Questions like that are great because they guide your focus without being too limiting. They invite exploration. Once you have a list of questions like these, you are ready to begin responding to them via freewriting.

You just go from one question to the next, responding and following your sense for the mysteries behind the questions. The exercise is about putting yourself on the spot. You give answers to the questions even if they aren't the perfect ones or the correct ones.

To keep things flowing through the list, give yourself one minute to answer each question. Feel free to rove back and forth if you need to.

As you might have guessed, the Hot Seat Exercise is great when you are in a real pinch for time. There's nothing quite like a deadline to get you motivated. This exercise takes you out of the paralysis of perfectionism and procrastination and gets you to take action.

You can implement this however you want. The simplest approach would be to write out by hand or draft the questions in your text editor, Scrivener or Word or whatever, and set a timer to go off every couple of minutes.

You can also do it with a voice recorder if you have recording software such as Audacity, Ableton, Bitwig, Logic or similar. Basically you can just record an audio file that is the duration you want to freewrite for, and cue up yourself reading the questions at the specified intervals. To begin the freewrite, you press play, and you hear yourself read the first question. Two minutes in, you hear yourself read the second question. And so forth. You get to be your own moderator in a debate, or the hiring manager in a job interview.

You could also do the opposite, start with the questions written down then speak your timed response into a voice recorder or transcription software for you to work with later.

So, let's look at some example questions.

> My purpose is
> My purpose is not
> My gut sense for this chapter is . . .
> This piece/book/article is written for X, is about Y
> This piece/book/article is not written for X, is not about Y
> What I'm really hoping/trying/need to say here
> What else can I see here?
> How can I boil this down in a couple of sentences?
> What really matters about this?
> What am I not seeing here?
> What have I not said that is absolutely vital?

Your questions can follow a linear progression, or they can be random.

Questions like these get you to dig deeper towards the center of yourself and your project. They ground you and challenge you.

Seed crystals

Analogies are more powerful than rocket fuel.

Analogies are very often the best ways to remember things and to connect with the logic behind them. They have a versatility that mere data or descriptive facts lack. When you understand an analogy behind something, you gain access to its depth in a way that can be reverse engineered.

You are probably familiar with cubic zirconia, which is a synthetic diamond that they make in a lab. From what I understand about making synthetic crystals, they start with a small crystal and they do something to that crystal. They dissolve it in a solution and from that solution somehow they work their magic to grow a larger crystal around that center one.

You can apply the analogy of a seed crystal as a model in your writing.

By starting with the concept of something, you can expand outward from it through freewriting. Simply hold the concept in mind and then write without stopping, allowing yourself to follow threads and tangents then return to the main idea.

How To Apply This: The Life Calling Exercise

One way to apply this technique is to hold a really big concept in mind and write without stopping to explore it until your time runs out.

A big topic such as "What do I feel is my life calling right now?" is one that you can stick with for hours, never really exhausting all the things you can list and explore and detail. You might find yourself writing about how you want to travel to Bora Bora, and maybe you get lost in the sensory descriptions that evokes when you really think about doing it.

To recenter and get back to relevance, all you have to do is return to the main question, the center point of the writing exercise: "What do I feel is my life calling right now?" And maybe that will get you to thinking about what kind of relationships you want to have, and why, and how they might come about. You can keep going and going with this exercise. In fact, you might find that the longer you spend at it, the richer the experience.

Allow yourself to restate things when you are uncertain about how to proceed. You already said it one way, so try saying it a different way. What does the same thing look like from a different perspective or vantage point? What does it feel like when you invoke it again? How might someone else rephrase it?

Each time you repeat something, you repeat it into a new moment. It will feel somewhat different. Things are not only one way. Generally, the way something first appears to us leaves a lot still mysterious and unexplored. What often happens is that we think we are expressing everything clearly and there's no other way to say it than the way we already have.

Experience has taught me that it's often true that there is still a lot packed away that might want to be seen. It's not about reiterating things mechanically. It's about feeling things out and trusting the process. Just as with any freewriting, you don't have to keep everything you write.

The process will reveal more facets to your topic as you restate things. While you are writing, it might feel like you are restating the same thing, in looking back through later you will probably find that you are actually showing really different nuances of something that even if the first way you said it was the best way to say it, you have a more thorough understanding and ownership of the kernel idea.

A Bit About Purpose

Even in the most free-flowing writing sessions, there is always a purpose. That purpose might be a simple (and bold) desire to explore language, to see what happens, to engage in some self-discovery and experiment with words. Very often, you'll find you hold a sense of purpose related to an outcome you desire. Generally, when you write something, you have at least some idea of what you are writing towards.

One way to arrive at clarity about purpose is to ask the question 'where does this writing belong?' In my journal? In what section? Does this material belong to my memoir project? That mystery novella I have been thinking about? Do I need this to be in front of a wide audience of readers on social media?

When you know your purpose, you have that much more to rest on during your sojourn through the wild terrain of the imagination. It can make all the difference between a frustrating meander and a well-timed expedition.

A Bit About Audience

It's no small consideration to know who your intended reader is. When I say "intended reader," I mean the living breathing human on the other end of the page from where you work.

I don't think of audience in terms of market segment. My actual readers are real people, so my intended reader is a real person too. Real people can't be reduced to mere members of a given category. I think of my readers in terms of feelings and shared values.

I try to focus on giving them what they want. I speak to what we have in common – what we are working towards, what we love. I try to feel things through their perspective.

For a stranger to become my reader for any significant duration, they need to know, like, and trust me. I have to earn that from them. That's on my mind when I am writing. I want to hook them, and not just at the beginning, but all the way through. I want them to be ongoingly compelled by what I write. I want to honor their expectations and at the same time give them something different, something new.

My hope is to give them something that charms or sparks them into letting go of what they wanted before they showed up now that the experience is happening. I want to give them what they want and also remove all limits.

Audience is of paramount importance. As is true with purpose, you really want to know as much about your audience as you can. The more you know, the more considerate you can be in your writing. The more you can empathize with the reader, the better you can speak their language. The practice of putting yourself in the shoes of your reader gives you a useful perspective on your own writing.

And even if your audience is yourself, it still pays off to be attentive to this component. If you're writing in a journal that only you will ever read, you can still do things based on how you know yourself that will make it easier on you. Organization, for example. Dating entries, adding headers when it feels appropriate. If you are feeling especially considerate to the Future You, you could even do crazy things like add a table of contents. I mean, how helpful would that be for you if, ten years down the road, you find some dusty journal and have zero recollection of what it contains? I have certainly had the experience of going through old notebooks to find them impenetrable, labyrinthine, cluttered, no idea what to do with any of it.

The last thing you want is to have hidden gems in your writing that never see the light of day because you didn't give enough consideration for the expectations of your audience when you wrote it.

Let's say you just penned your first novel ever, and you release it into the world. That book might contain some of the most exquisite material the world has ever seen, but if you don't get it in front of the right reader and you don't present things in a way that stems from an understanding of how that reader needs things to be, few will be able to appreciate it.

As with anything else, the concern about audience isn't something that should constrict your ability to be inspired or prevent you from writing. You don't need to know everything before you begin. You can refine as you go. Just as relationships change over time, the experience of freewriting deepens and shifts your understanding about your reader and yourself.

Why It's Good to Work Against Time

The freewriting exercises in this book are often timed, which is to say, you work against a tight deadline, measured in minutes and seconds. The idea is to make the most of a small window, to cram as much intensity as you can into it. We begin by doing short intense sprints of writing, then move on to writing marathons, ideally with the same level of intensity.

There's always going to be some limiting factor towards meeting your writing goals and staying on track with your long-term vision [examples include energy, not having ideas, other responsibilities, shifts in focus, losing motivation in your goal, etc].

When time is the source of your constraint, it removes you as the source of the bottleneck, for one thing. That in itself is a relief. There's a time to work and a time to let go.

Working against time creates a very straightforward playing field for you to operate. Anyone can block out some time, whether it is twenty minutes or two hours or whatever. Don't believe me? Time yourself the next time you pop onto social media. You probably intended to log on to do one simple thing. Next thing you know, twenty minutes have passed, and you have completely lost your sense of clarity and motivation. At least, this is what I notice in myself. That's a big reason why I no longer have a Facebook account: it was a time and energy drain. Even if everything else in my life remained the same, simply by trimming that out, I gained a lot more time and actually freed up some clarity in my day-to-day stuff.

Working against time creates an organic sense of urgency because you have a mini-deadline. Maybe you can't accomplish all your lifelong dreams in your single twenty minute freewriting session, but you can accomplish a great deal, perhaps more than in two hours of normal interruption-prone writing.

And if you're able to borrow that same functionality when writing for eight hours, things begin to get very interesting. . .

Expectations for Timed Freewriting Sessions

what can Happen During a 20 Minute Freewrite?

What is achievable for you in twenty minutes? Well, one possibility is that you can jot out the fundamentals of your life work in such a way that makes the next five years of your life a hundred times clearer. In twenty minutes you can experience the breakthrough of a lifetime. Stranger things have happened.

Of course, it's not always going to be like that. It's healthy to hold no limits on how much can happen while at the same time not judging that the experience will mean failure if something unexpected happens. It's important to set the bar where it's challenging but not soul-crushingly difficult, otherwise you're setting yourself up for disappointment even if you accomplish a lot.

The question to ask here is what you would like to achieve during your freewrite. And instead of setting only one goal, why not account for varying degrees of success? Maybe you want to draft an article but you also want to be open for two or three article outlines to come about during the next twenty minute freewrite. Then, whether you get only the one article or all three (or more), you set yourself up for success.

What Can Happen During A Two Hour Freewrite?

Short answer: A lot. Largely it depends on how clear you are and how fast you write. 1000-2000 words per hour is a respectable average rate. Word count is not the only way of measuring success, but it is an easy one to measure.

My advice is not to expect yourself to accomplish everything in a single pass but to nevertheless have clear plans about what you can focus on during any given freewrite. When you look at the example of nanowrimo, you can see how it is achievable for many people to draft a novel in a month. There are loads of people who have shared their experiences with this.

If, for example, your goal is to write 50,000 words in a month, how many writing sessions will it take for you to get there? If you know your larger word count goal, see how it lines up with hourly goals. You can map out how many sessions you will spend to meet your big goal. Amazingly high words counts can also be possible in a burst of an hour or two. If you really are jazzed on your material, maybe you can even sustain that for longer. A whole lot can happen in two hours.

See what happens when you set a huge word count goal for your next two hour freewrite. If you find the challenge inspiring, spend the next two hours firing away on your keyboard and see what emerges. Just as important, be present to how it feels. After you're done with that and you have reviewed your material, if you found the session effective, spend some time planning your next burst to tweak what worked best.

Often it only takes really small shifts to make all the difference. For example, you might realize that it would be more helpful for you to have a more rigorous understanding of some of your characters or some of the worldbuilding elements. Then, if you have the energy for it, go for another two hour burst to generate material along those lines.

One healthy option here is to take a short break where you do a very different activity, ideally something outdoors that is physically engaging. Go for a workout. Have a conversation with a friend about something totally different. After a huge burst of productivity, amazing things can happen if you switch gears. For example, you can plan a call with a friend to explore ideas or brainstorm. Instead of having no ideas or feeling drained, you may find that you have primed the pump and things can easily flow.

Because you have pushed yourself and given yourself a major success, you have banished the toxic sense of "I can't" that plagues most of us so much of the time. The secret formula for taking breaks:

1. Switch gears physically, spatially and mentally
2. Briefly assess your writing and make adjustments. Jot out a sketch
3. Give yourself another two-hour success

This is how virtuous circles are born.

Other Goal Types

Another type of goal, this one completely unrelated to word count, can be based on how developed you want your content to be. "Finish this article in one hour," for example.

Or you can set a number of elements you want to generate. "In one hour, I will come up with 100 ways to innovate our business strategy."

Be flexible about mode but clear about intent. If you need to, or if it would support your writing session, feel free to make a rapid transition to voice dictation from typing, or from handwriting to typing. You'd be surprised how fruitful small changes can be. Even changes as small as going from standing to sitting, or even sitting in a different spot in the same room. Sitting in a different room. Going outside, working around people versus working alone for awhile. Moving from handwriting mode to typewritten mode, you can choose to switch projects or work on the same project. Sometimes these natural changes support switching modalities. If you are writing by hand as you write your life goals, and then you make the transition to begin typing, you might find that you no longer feel like writing goals, but instead feel inspired to write poetry or describe in vivid detail your immediate surroundings.

The unspoken foundational goal is that you freewrite regardless of what happens, so even if you make a complete departure from your original designs, you will still succeed as long as you continue to write.

There is a great deal to be said for going where inspiration takes you. However, this is also a case where it is important to be aware of your own unique tendencies for getting off topic. Might you feel the pull to write poetry because you are avoiding something that is worthwhile about your goal writing? Or are you genuinely inspired and it would be a tragedy to remain rigid in the face of that?

When in doubt, just go with what feels the most vital and alive. If you end up following a whim that turns out to be nothing more than a distraction from where the heart of your writing session lies, simply do what you can to return to relevance as you are able.

It's a risk to follow yourself down different avenues of creative possibility, but it's a risk worth taking. A few sessions where you really allow yourself to do this can habituate you to a larger standpoint of creative sponteneity. Even if some of the sessions don't turn out perfectly, in the long term you may be surprised how easily new ideas come to you.

In the big picture of things, the trust you have of the process gives you better and more subtle navigational skills with respect to choosing which ideas to pursue. Really, there is no need to force the useless impulses away as long as you maintain an overall focus on the context and intent of your project.

Maybe, for example, a seemingly irrelevant or distracting mode of description turns out to be something you can use later in a novel. Maybe you can discover a different perspective on your subject or a different style for how you describe things. Even if the material itself isn't useful, you might very well be broadening your proficiency or gaining a different writerly skill.

What matters most isn't what you do but how you engage with it.

In my life, I have improved as a writer by experiencing life and trying my hand at other art forms. By becoming more perceptive as a visual artist, I improved as a writer. Through my experiences as a meditator, I cleared away much of the cloudiness and murkiness that definitely interferes with clear thinking and with my true voice showing up on the page.

Not all that we write is gold. But we don't become better writers only when we write gold. I believe that writers improve when they:

- take risks that they can win at
- do anything that moves them towards greater vulnerability and realness as a person
- are devoted to their practice, not only by putting more words on the page, but specifically by doing so with a sense of sponteneity, immediacy, transparency.

With this kind of improvement, the writing becomes holographic to the writer's state of being at the time that they were writing it. That is to say, their writing offers an experience that can be re-entered in a very tangible sense. Therefore, the reader can get a better feel for the writer's true self, and not just the ways that the writer has learned to write from school or imitating other writing.

What About When You Don't Feel Like It?

The practice of freewriting brings many opportunities to be aware of the subtle shifts that happen within your own energy level and quality of focus.

And sometimes, you don't feel like writing.

When should you get yourself to write anyway and when should you take a break?

Overall, the ambition I want to encourage here is to condition yourself to be able to comfortably write for long stretches without stopping. Other than that, it's ultimately about what you want. It's your practice, you're driving the vehicle, so you call the shots.

As a suggestion, here is a simple rule: Write when the energy is there and take a break when you're ready to take a break. Make the break a restorative one. Keep the distractions and the in-between time to a minimum. Commit to what you want to commit to and also allow yourself to be a human. Just don't let things get too complicated. Stick with what you've chosen to do.

A question to ask at any given moment: Am I really putting my best interests at the forefront? What part of me is really in charge here? When I don't feel like it, is that just some part of me reaching for an excuse?

As an example, one aspiring freewriter might convince themselves that they don't feel like writing only to find themselves drawn to kill a half hour on Reddit, after which point they don't feel any better and they haven't gotten any closer to their writing goals. As a contrast, what if that person who, feeling lackluster, simply paused where they were, closed their eyes, felt more deeply within themselves, asking to be reminded about some glimmer or spark of desire about writing? Maybe that's all that needs to happen. Not only can it be that simple, at some level it really needs to be kept simple. Once you're in touch with something that deeply motivates you, you're unstoppable. Everyone has this capability within them.

As a training, it's good to rely on other factors besides fatigue or boredom or distraction to dictate whether you are doing what you want or not.

"If I write when I don't feel like it, then won't I write crap?" Maybe. But in my own experience, it's still totally possible to write gold, even to be completely unaware that what you're writing is the best thing ever. I have written great material when I started the session in a foul mood. What matters most isn't the grumpy part of you, but the part of you that deeply cares and wants to engage their writing ability at deeper and deeper levels.

If you really are afraid that what you write won't be any good, sticking with the process creates the best opportunity to work through it towards something better. Just as when moving toward any goal, there will be times when you don't think you can do it or don't feel you can do it. You have to press past those times. They may just be a sign that you are going farther than before, so take that discomfort or fear or disorientation as a good thing.

With every action you take, you are always supporting one thing or another, one set of habits or another. Find what works for you that supports your energy and presses you towards your goal. It's a practice that always merits being sensitive about. You don't want to burn yourself out, but you don't want to slouch off, either. If you burn out, you won't reach your goals because you'll be too fried to get out of bed, or maybe you'll meet your goals technically but not in spirit. On the other hand, slouch around and you won't meet your goals, or if you do, it'll take thirty times as long, and the writing you manifest will lack oomph and clarity.

What I'm driving at here is really an opportunity for self-leadership. You have your long term vision, and you're the one who is going to hold yourself to it. But it can feel like a long journey between here and there. Besides having the vision in the first place, two main things are required. It's important to be flexible and sensitive:

- Sensitive to feel where you really are (and be honest).

- Flexible to adapt your process so that it works for you, meets your needs, and keeps you on track.

Bird's Eye Mode – Pattern Recognition

Bird's Eye Mode (sometimes called High Elevation Mode) gives you the ability to view your written work from a more stepped-back perspective. This is helpful when writing longer works so that you can see the forest for the trees and know how to properly pace things.

I used to run into issues where I would get 70 percent through with the draft of a novel and then something would call my attention to the beginning of the book. I would write a new first chapter. And maybe then I would write another first chapter, this one occurring just prior to the previous first chapter.

It sounds maddening, but on a science fiction trilogy I was drafting, I literally wrote the whole first book nearly entirely backwards. What used to be chapter one later fell toward the end of the book. The process was grueling to say the least.

Changing the way a story begins completely shifts the stakes for the rest of the book. I learned a lot about messing with story structure from doing this, but it was about the toughest slog imaginable. If I were to go back and do it again, I would have done things one of two ways:

- I would have finished the draft, and only then gone back to change things with the beginning. The way things turned out, it would have worked fine. I could have written that book and then written the next book as a prequel to it.

- I would have spent more time in the high elevation phase really making sure I was happy with the flow of events. In the high elevation view of the book I could have seen the missing pieces and it would have been much easier to change things, since the draft had not already been written. It's much easier to cut a character if that character doesn't actually exist yet.

How to Engage High Elevation When Freewriting

As with other freewriting, this technique is flexible. Each writing project – and each writing session – is unique. The main idea with high elevation mode is to work in an organizational capacity. The material you generate is not important in terms of its exact wording but rather how the words and phrases can symbolize larger organizational structures within your project. Chapter headings, significant topics and scenes, and so forth. So, keep things simple and don't get too attached to any specific goings-on.

Use Questions to Navigate

One of the best ways to navigate as you freewrite is to be strategic with the way you ask yourself questions.

Questions are all you need to drive the most profound creative discoveries. Questions – especially simple ones – are powerful. The way we ask questions impacts what happens for us.

Before you begin freewriting, and then periodically during your freewrite, ask questions about the big picture. When you get an idea for a scene, look down at the scene from above, so to speak. Jot it down, focusing on what most energizes you about that idea.

Drop any expectation that pulls you towards the need to resolve any details or in-scene specifics. Once you have touched on the main elements of that scene, return to asking questions about the story's big picture. Rest on the high ideals of your piece.

You only need to begin to map the terrain. It is fine for things to be abstract, vague, or nonspecific. Move from general to specific without expecting that your specifics need to add up perfectly or click into place just yet. You're not on a road with only one way forward. You have complete mobility to move around as needed, shifting in any direction to better see the lay of the land.

If you're writing a novel, then here is where you explore your character dynamics. What do your characters like and dislike, how do they differ from each other, and how do they feel about each other and various aspects of the world? As any specifics occur to you, you are free to write them down, but you are under no obligation to do so.

Engaging bird's eye mode, you are free to fly and flow wherever. Record the textures and feelings you are seeking to enact in your project. Rather than needing to nail things down before finding forward progress, the forward momentum is free-floating.

Though your writing goes from line to line, your flow of thoughts can flit from the beginning of your story to the end, from one character to another. Instead of needing to sketch out scenes or map out any dialogue, your job in bird's eye mode is to stay at the high elevation view where general begins to become specific.

The more you engage this mode, the more clarity you have on things like:

- The effect you want to create
- The general ordering of events
- The dynamics between elements such as settings and characters
- The textures and flavors of the main parts of your story

Writing this way has the effect of producing several useful buckets where you can later put things. Because you have mapped things out, you have a sense for how things feel in the beginning, middle and end, and how each character brings their own qualities to the arena. When you later want to draft further, this material can organically find its rightful home.

At this stage, nothing is anywhere close to being set in stone, of course. There will be room to adjust as you move ahead. The benefit of this freewriting modality is that it gives you ownership of the whole terrain. You gain a sense of order and command over your material, and from that high-elevation mastery, you can feel more at ease when it comes time to draft each element in earnest down at ground level.

You could think of high elevation mode as like using notecards to plot an outline or build a storyboard. If you have ever made storyboards for a book or film, your expertise will come in handy here. What you are seeking to capture with this exercise is a glimpse into the key moments of different parts of your written piece.

How to Revise From A High Elevation

The high elevation or bird's eye view can be implemented during the rereading or revising process in a variety of ways.

Essentially, the way to apply it when looking at a previous freewrite is to comb through it and look for things that are potentially interesting, usable, or unfinished – anything that could provide useful forward momentum. It doesn't matter if it is out of order or unclear.

The useful material is collected as if each part fit in with the other like elements in a mind map. It's nonlinear, so you may find it more intuitive to do this longhand on a piece of paper or using writing software such as Scrivener that can easily accommodate for moving around material. The material is brought forward with the understanding that it offers only a distant glimpse of some aspect of what the eventual piece might be.

You can think of these pieces as headers, but more accurately they are fragments. A header generally bears the responsibility that it has to state in basic summary form what the body material will be about. However, in bird's eye mode, you don't have to do this. The fragment might be a header, or more likely it might simply offer a clue, a glimpse into some key aspect of that part of the novel.

If, for example, you were developing a bird's eye view of the end of *The Lord of the Rings*, the chapter might eventually be about the quest to Mount Doom, but the glimpse might be a final confrontation with Smeagol. It's not only about the Smeagol confrontation; it's also about everything that happens before and after that confrontation. But that was the glimpse afforded to you in your freewrite, so that is what you use to move forward with. You can build around that fragment in both forwards and reverse until what you have starts to look more like a rough outline.

Module 3 Recap

Be sure to give each of the following at least a couple of tries before moving on:

- High Elevation
- Life Calling
- Hot Seat Mode

Module 4: Multiply Your Ideas

In this module we will cover techniques that bring in some organizational strategies specifically as a means to take new ideas and make them bigger, branch them outward into new divergent nodes. We will also look at some ways to implement talking-writing and the power of using questions to unlock door after door. But first let's touch on one of the cornerstones of this endeavor to freewrite with depth, which is to embrace fertile chaos.

Fertile chaos, The Stuff of Life

> *It is not the critic who counts; not the man who points out how the strong man stumbles, or where the doer of deeds could have done them better. The credit belongs to the man who is actually in the arena, whose face is marred by dust and sweat and blood; who strives valiantly; who errs, who comes short again and again, because there is no effort without error and shortcoming; but who does actually strive to do the deeds; who knows great enthusiasms, the great devotions; who spends himself in a worthy cause; who at the best knows in the end the triumph of high achievement, and who at the worst, if he fails, at least fails while daring greatly, so that his place shall never be with those cold and timid souls who neither know victory nor defeat.*
>
> - Theodore Roosevelt

Chaos is not the enemy of creation. It is a sign of it.

Deep freewriting is about taking the plunge. It is intended for any person who wants to get more in touch with themselves, their creativity, to become a more creative person, to become more of who they really are. When you do a writing marathon, you learn to redirect your thinking so that you are in touch with inspiration.

As with any intense experience, the idea is that you – anyone– can simply do it and become a different person on the other side.

You don't need to identify as a "writer." You simply need to agree to follow through with the activities.

Deep freewriting will open doors for you. Not only will it give you a lot of material, it will also help you process things. It gives you leaping-off points for more areas to explore.

People have been taught and praised for writing in a way that is stiff and correct but dead. It's dead because there is no risk-taking, no wildness, no sense of spontaneity. We have become fearful of the chaos of creation.

When you sit down and affirm that you are going to write without stopping for a length of time, especially a long time – you step into something bigger. It's courageous. It's risky. It's out of the box, out of the ordinary. You don't know what's on the other side.

These writing habits take you somewhere. The world doesn't really demand of everyone to really dive into their depth, but if there is a part of you that says yes to the idea, you do yourself a service to give it your best.

Writing is not like any other media. On the one hand, it's more complicated. It's also more intuitive for most people. Writing creates a symbolic record just by doing it. You can scan your writing and travel through time, through the moments that were there for you the various present moments that were alive for you when you write each and every word. Writing is immensely versatile and so it gets tied to many other things. It also gets burdened by a lot of judgment that it is all correct and polished.

We use writing for creative reasons and also to pass information, and when we freewrite, we also use writing as a modality for personal exploration. It's a process that stirs things up. Writing gets you into a unique flow state where thinking and feeling sort of merge.

Our conditioning prevents us from a worthwhile and spontaneous relationship with our inner landscape and the imagination. My aim is to convey a sense of mystery about the chaos of creation and to show you more ways of getting the critic out of the way.

As you freewrite, be a vessel for experience. Be present and let your natural voice hone itself. Experience will bring you your own discoveries.

Expect the unexpected.

Exercise: Rewrite To Enter the Same Space

Think of "space" as being equivalent to the overall feeling or vibe of a book, a character, a scene, or any piece of writing. The term is useful when writing becomes more about the experience and less about concepts or ideas.

When writers get stuck, it is often because they are trying to wrestle with things at the level of rigid concepts or ideas. This stuckness can be circumvented by choosing a different way of navigation, to trust your gut, to feel your way along, to taste your way through your writing. The space of a given piece of writing might be thought of as its room, a place where all its textures and associations live. When you feel a piece's space as a whole separate layer from the ideas, actions, and plots it might contain, you have the ability to be more free about how to work with all its particulars.

For this exercise, you start with a previously written piece of yours, whether finished or unfinished.

1. Read through it to get a feel for it.
2. Set it aside.

3. Rewrite it. Write your way back into the space of the piece and set out on a similar trajectory. Don't worry about writing it better. The impulse here is to set out with the intention to write your way into the same space. You don't have to hit all the same points or even to rewrite it in a way that anyone else would recognize. If you end up taking a completely different trajectory, that's fine. Again, it's not about repeating what you already wrote, only about entering its space and resonating with the way it feels.

Other Options and Ideas

- Write a "deleted scene" to the piece, something extra and nonessential. In your writing, have a discussion with yourself or someone else about it.
- Reflect and express what you feel about the old draft. This process might unlock something, either for being able to reconcile that draft or for future writing.
- Ask questions that examine the assumptions and beliefs around that writing.
- Describe the world it's a part of.
- If it is an unfinished draft, can you write something now to freshen up the material? Bring it up to speed with where you are now, where the world is now? What happens when you blend your past efforts with your present efforts?

Exercise: Write Into Someone Else's Space

For this one, find a selection of someone else's writing and freewrite into that space.

Find a written piece by someone else that you find engaging. Picture yourself sitting around a table where one person told a tale. Finished, they point at you. Now it's your turn to stand on the table and continue the tale. Everyone in the room is OK with whatever you say, wherever it goes. Consider yourself a contemporary, a local, a peer.

Possibilities for what shape your writing is to take:

- Fan fiction or a tale-within-a-tale.
- Your own tale from that part of you that loves and knows the space of that other writing.
- Remix or spin their piece into a different genre – you'll take a novel and write a poem into the same space.
- Maybe the space of someone else's poem will inspire you to do some research or reflection or to describe the world as seen from within that poem.

Exercise: Feel Your Goals

OK, so you have visions and goals. This exercise is an opportunity to take some time to feel them out. You don't need to make any decisions right now or plan anything. Just allow your feelings – not only your thoughts – to be here and give oomph and specificity to what can happen now and in the future.

Let's say you're facing a lot of uncertainty around your current car situation. You are paying too much for your existing car, and you don't enjoy driving it anymore. You want to exchange it for a cheaper one that you would actually enjoy more. You feel strange about this. It's a goal about which you feel conflicted.

Freewriting is great for exploring conflicts big and small. You don't have to decide where to put your conflicts. You just let them all be there in their rawness. You feel this, you feel that, and you don't have to separate things into categories of problems versus solutions. Let all the tangled thoughts get aired out, let all the emotions get felt, let all the beliefs get expressed and seen.

Explore the feelings and let the sparks fly until some catharsis is reached. If feel like it and you still have time, see if you can keep going anyway, after experiencing a release. Who knows, maybe there is more to be discovered. Though if you persist and it feels flat, then there's no need to force anything.

Optional Step: Move From Feelings Into Action

Now that you have aired out your feelings on the matter, you can choose to move from feelings into action.

Sticking with the feelings rather than rationalizations, map out a written sort of flow chart, something like:

- If I do this, then these are my options.
- If I do this, then these are my options.
- If A, it feels like this. If B, it feels this way.

You aren't obligated to do this phase, and even if you do, it doesn't lock you into any action. Doing it simply helps to map things out so you can be more strategic about your choices.

Things to watch for:

- Following whims and justifying them.
- Losing touch of the ground.
- Rigid emotionality.

It's not about convincing yourself one way or the other. Trying to persuade yourself will not help reach clarity. Instead, try to represent things – including feelings– how they are, moving towards being matter-of-fact.

Exercise: Speak-Revision

This exercise is to be used for material that you have drafted using your voice by speaking.

To do this exercise, listen to a recording of yourself speaking and write what you are noticing that isn't explicitly being stated. The idea is to focus not on the words but on the way that the words were spoken. The nuance passed by voice can be fruitful to honor during revision.

A few options:

- Play the audio all the way through and transcribe what you literally said. Then go back through, feel for the nuances, and make any additions or adjustments in the written text.
- Play the audio and pause it every so often, restating each recorded passage in a way that better conveys your intent.

Writing and speaking can bring very different experiences. The directness of words on a page carries something that voice doesn't. It's very true that voice can accomplish a million textural miracles that can be difficult or impossible to really replicate using letters on the page.

You can think of this as a way to feel the way that the voice naturally, effortlessly, performs something that the literal words do not. The performance does not need to be intentional. It is there regardless of whether it was intended simply by the fact that the words have been spoken.

It is good to be mindful of the space behind the literal words. Feel the impetus, the environment around the communication. What else gets transmitted? It may be very subtle. This might very well be felt during the pauses and silences. What isn't being said in any given moment?

Or, you may find that when you speak the dialogue belonging to a given character, you are speaking in a different quality of voice. It would be good to ask whether you are conveying the sense of that tonality in the text alone.

To be clear, this exercise is not about assessing the way you were speaking or what you did or didn't say. It's simply a practice to feel for the unspoken nuances that can easily exist in a voice when speaking aloud. To really convey these nuances might require rewording what was said or adding or subtracting some of your writing.

Exercise: Navigate By Association

You've heard about the psychoanalytical technique of free association, used famously by Freud. I'm no expert, but my understanding is that one fundamental of free association where you hear a word or phrase then respond with whatever word or phrase that first comes to mind.

Free association brings interesting possibilities for the freewriter, perhaps stemming from the interesting coincidence that it is also considered a "free" activity.

This is a great exercise to keep handy for longer freewriting sessions when you might yourself apt to go blank. If you feel yourself about to struggle or get frustrated, try this instead: look at the last word you wrote and take it as an invitation to do a free association. Then do the same with that word. And the next, until you feel like writing about something else.

It can be a very dynamic exercise. You might surprise yourself.

The goal here is not only to keep things moving, but also to end up someplace new. To mix the pot, basically. Dig a little deeper and enter the mystery with a sense of spontaneity.

It helps steer clear of inner judgment, since there is no way of getting free association "correct."

It might look like this:

> Giraffe trombone aljazeera rainbow zebra ukelele dancer
> alphabet Madagascar fruit salad fruit bowl fruitcake
> cheesecake lift kit motor oil rain dance concrete jungle
> dank mastery reach high look low

It should suffice to do this for a few minutes. No need to go overly nuts with it.

The thing with this as with most any exercise is to actually be willing to do it when you feel blocked. It's helpful to have options when the time comes, things you don't have to think about or look for. Something that is light and easy and ready at hand. This fits the bill.

It may lend you some ideas but mainly what it does is works things behind the scenes. Besides keeping you in the flow of language and keeping you out of a more familiar space of frustration, it offers you the chance to dive around and end up someplace else.

Another option for tweaking: Instead of doing just one or two words, try making a free associated phrase that is three words long (or more).

Whatever limit you set, keep yourself at at limit. If you choose three words, stick with three words but no more. And remember, keep it as free as possible. Make no effort at crafting it. Just work your improv muscle and let it come and go.

> Sam says hi. Willy wakes friday. Early walkers catapult.
> Day dancing dirty. Catio daybed daybreak. Sal takes
> walks. Iggy spaces in. Hidalgo dojo trampoline.

And so forth.

Yet another option: Before you start writing, pre-load some topics into your association pachinko machine.

Write down a list of jumping-off words to free associate from and keep that list somewhere nearby. When you feel stuck, pull some material from the page and use it in your free association. Pull the same material several times if you like and see what happens by virtue of repetition or by weaving similar turns of phrase.

The point is, the exercise is malleable. With freewriting as with anything creative, I want to encourage you to be flexible and see everything as customizable, something you can tweak. Try it first the "official" way and see how it goes.

Free association definitely showed itself to be a welcome addition to my 24 hour writing marathon. I didn't even start with any real idea of what I wanted to write about, and I committed to 24 hours of that uncertainty. The free association exercise emerged organically out of the flow that I was in.

Technique: Trees From Tens

James Altucher has a great daily habit of writing down a list of ten things. The ambition behind this exercise is to become what he calls an Idea Machine. Ideas, he says, are becoming the new currency. So the more we can produce good ideas, the more we can stay valuable.

I did this exercise for a few months myself each morning and I really liked it. The goal of the exercise is to create a list of ten things. It doesn't really matter what the list is. It could be ten ways to make more money, ten romantic things to do with your lover, ten types of writing instruments. Coming up with lists gets you engaged and flexes your ability to find new possibilities.

My suggestion for you is to use freewriting to come up with a list of ten things. Then, once you have your list, you can further branch outward from some or all of the items on the list, making a list of additional subcategories for each list item.

So, for this exercise, the goal is to create a list, then to magnify that list into multiple lists. Freewrite to develop your list. During your freewrite, you can number or otherwise mark each list item as it occurs to you. When you aren't sure where to go next, simply continue writing until you arrive at the next one.

As you write, ask yourself questions to look for opportunities to show things from a different perspective.

For example: How would my uncle Mike say that? What else could be said about this?

Let it be an ongoing discussion with yourself as you map out your tree of ideas.

Exercise

- Freewrite to come up with ten things.
- When you have come up with at least ten, read back through what you have and order the ten things into a fairly concise list.
- Looking at this list, begin a second round of freewriting so that you find at least two items that will fit under each of the ten items in the original list.
- When you have at least twenty items, read back through and order them into the same list, with each of the new items nested underneath the original list.
- Freewrite one more time, exploring at least two new items to fit within each subcategory.
- When you have forty new items, order them into the same list.

In a short amount of time, you have generated a fairly well-structured list with lots of subcategories.

Now, what to do with this list?

Freewrite, of course! The specifics of how to work with your list really depends on what your list is about. Let's say you were making a list of scenes you wanted to have in a story. You can take that and use it as the beginning of an outline or sketch for your story, using it to freewrite further material.

The Writing Relay

Variety is the spice of life. Monotony isn't. It's especially beneficial to mix things up when you are in a stagnant place imaginatively and feeling a bit dull physically or energetically.

This exercise brings about a shake-up that can lead to breakthroughs. Yeah, you can sit there and fight with yourself. You can keep plodding away. There's nothing wrong with that. But sometimes it's important to disrupt yourself. By moving energy and engaging the flow, you're sure to shake things up and gain a different perspective.

Here's how to do a writing relay:

- Write for five minutes
- Hop up and do five minutes of physical exercise
- Rest for a minute to catch your breath
- Review your writing
- Write for another five minutes, repeating the process

Different Registers

The word "register" can mean different things. I use the word here to refer to voices we use which differ depending on our purpose. As I'm describing it here, there is an intrinsic connection between your purpose and the register you're writing in. When you're writing a simple note to yourself, your register is very different from when you're writing a love letter. The purpose is different and so the voice you bring to the page is very different.

Examples of registers from my own experience would be:

- administrative-type writing. The voice here is efficient, dry, and only about actionables
- motivating myself
- the voice of a character in a story

- narrator's voice

Generally different registers each have a few things that they are particularly suited for. The administrative register is a great way to take quick notes, but a bad match for a love poem, so it is important to bring some awareness to the different ways that we write. If you are having difficulty writing something, it is possible that you can find an entry point by feeling into the component parts that add up to that given register. Simply being aware what register you are writing in provides handy organization during a freewrite. It's also something you can use to group out different sections when you go back through and reread something you freewrote.

The suggestion here is to do something in your document to make each different register discernable. This can be as simple as using white space – just leave a blank line whenever you notice that you are switching registers.

You may find the process interesting and even somewhat enlightening to see how it feels natural to go from register to register. Sometimes what appears like writer's block is really just a need to shift flow. Let yourself be drawn towards whatever register you feel compelled to write in.

Another way to think about this technique is as if you're borrowing from the art of collage. Basically, by leaving yourself blank space around different registers, you can more easily distinguish and separate them (if you want) later. You can reorder all of the similar material into their own documents and – who knows – maybe with a little effort, you will have a masterpiece on your hands.

Sift Through A Question From Multiple Perspectives

This exercise is for when you want to discover original ways of resolving a problem or shedding light on a situation. It might be something you have thought so much about that you no longer feel like you can see the issue clearly. Or, maybe you have the desire to find a win-win amidst a complicated interpersonal situation. Or of course, you can use the exercise to work out something sticky about a story you're writing.

Write for ten minutes about something you don't understand, a scene, or an issue you want to tackle. Write about the problem. Write like you're speaking to yourself or thinking aloud.

- Reread. Familiarize yourself with the high points of what you wrote. Are there any juicy spots?
- Next, rewrite, changing the audience you're writing it to. Now instead of writing it to yourself, write it to your intended reader.
- Repeat the exercise writing for a reluctant reader, someone skeptical in every way of your stance or scene.

In the first phase of this exercise, you create some space for yourself so that you are freer and have more perspective with the problem or question. Much of the time our ideas are cloudy simply because our minds are crowded with potential ideas. There are many possibilities, and the sheer volume of choices can create rough traffic. If your ideas seem cloudy, see what happens when you give them space or stirred the symbolic pot.

When you begin writing, you beckon everything that might fit towards a given center of gravity. It requires a bit of patience and curiosity about what emerges. Even if nothing gets solved right away, the process has begun.

When you reread what you wrote, you sift through for nuggets and let everything go that is murky or frustrated or unproductive.

No matter what you find, you are moving towards more clarity. The reward is not only in the finding. The search engages an aspect of will and determination. So, yes, even if your ten minute freewriting session didn't consist of wall-to-wall diamonds, you still have been presented with a selection of material. From that material, you can find some things that are more refined than the rest. That momentum towards refinement, as much as the ideas themselves, is what you bring forward to the next phase.

Then, when you return to writing, this time with your reader in mind, you step into your own authority. You manifest your author-ness. Your writing the second time around will be more direct and straightforward. It doesn't need to have all the answers, but you do have something.

When you're done, it's high time to take a step back and marvel. Remember where you began the process, which was a state of nonknowing and even complete confusion. In only a few minutes, this is what you have done. What else might be possible if you continue to work this way?

Module Recap

There were a lot of exercises in this module, which perhaps is to be expected, since the theme was about magnifying ideas. The idea is for you to try your hand at each of them and to take your pick of the ones that really speak to where you are and what you want to embrace at this phase.

- Write into the space of an existing draft, whether yours or someone else's (or both).
- Do the Trees From Tens exercise to expand and multiply one idea into numerous ones and explore interconnection.

- Write your goals from the standpoint of the emotions that you have around them. Optionally, see where the wisdom of those emotions can lead you.
- Try out a writing relay, modulating between being stationary and moving your body.
- Explore the rich world of dictation and voice recording with the Speak Revision exercise.
- Sift through a question from multiple perspectives, trying out different voices and registers as well.

Module 5: The Marathon

First off... Congratulations! You have made it this far and you want more. We will dive into several new techniques (including the writing marathon), a bouquet of inspiration, and more.

Since writing is not just an intellectual phenomenon but also an energetic one, it matters how we engage with our craft.

We share with our reader the energetic spaces we regularly engage with. The more we travel the terrain, the more we get a sense for our place there. We form patterns and relationships, shortcuts and more efficient ways of navigating the imagination. The more present we are with the reality of imaginative creation, the more our words can impart a sense of ease and a spirit of clarity.

That ease and clarity is bound to take different forms, depending on how your awareness is geared into the process. During my formative and unplanned 24-hour writing marathon, one of the modes I found myself writing in was, surprisingly, fables. Fairy-stories. In that unceasing forward momentum exploring imagination's landscape, flowing from one fragment of creation to the next, it often happened that I came up on some easily shapeable driftwood that I found I could easily shape into that very short story form, the fable. Fables have such an affinity with the oral tradition, they can so nimbly, even when heavy-handedly, be reordered, paused, or shifted around as you write it. As a form, it is light and very accessible. They don't necessarily require depth of detail, character background or excessive realism.

I find that writing fables is a way of engaging that playful space so that it feels like I am both telling the truth and fibbing. Both of those feel good in different ways, and if you want vitality in your writing, it's important to feel good when you freewrite. When it feels like hard work, there's no lubrication in the gears of cognition, so ideas don't flow as smoothly or with as much refinement.

Oh, The Possibilities!

As part of the voyage towards the writing marathon, I want to share more of my enthusiasm and convey a sense of the depth and breadth that might be possible by this method.

In essence, I believe that we're barely scratching the surface of what can be done with freewriting.

We are doing something many people never really get the chance to: we're exploring writing in its textures, feelings, and spaces.

The process itself churns us in a way that ordinary ways of writing can't hold a candle to. It moves us towards the real and away from judgment and interpretation, not because they're bad, but because we remain present to the experience.

Just as with a musician doing scales and playing experimental pieces, as freewriters, we are ongoingly self-forgiving while staying true to the task. Experience is our teacher. Nothing we write has to come out perfect immediately. Let's give space to the mystery of creation by being present and matter-of-fact.

We freewriters don't strive to be correct. We strive to be alive and spontaneous within the context we're setting. Playing a wrong note doesn't get you kicked out of the freewriter's orchestra. A wrong note gets heard and released just like all the other notes.

Organization and context

If I were playing guitar and I got a phone call, and then I went back to playing guitar, I might need to doodle around to find what I had just been playing. I wouldn't curse myself for needing to get back into the flow to remember where I left off. It takes a bit of playing around to be able to play it flawlessly.

Freewriting requires an act of will where you hold (loosely) the context of what you are doing. And holding that context, you let yourself really be present. Maybe something apparently unrelated will manifest. If so, you can see what that feels like as it happens. It's your call whether to follow a new direction or let it pass. This continual act of refinement is a big part of how freewriting helps writers improve.

You can use the sketch technique as an extension of how you hold in mind the overall context and intent behind what you're writing. You may want some organization for your ideas, so you can jot a high-elevation outline or sketch as you go. Nothing makes this as-you-go outline any less effective than an official outline that you begin to work on beforehand.

Your outline can work fine even if it isn't full and complete. Discovering new outline elements can be like seeing new branches on a tree. Once you have a limb, you have something you can trace outwards. There's nothing that says you can't discover other limbs while you're up there climbing in the canopy. In an outline, it's good to discern which are limbs and which are leaves. Limbs would be the more supportive elements of the outline and the leaves would be the bits that can go here or there.

Even if you already have an outline, sketching one out as you go can help you to discern whether all the elements that feel most alive belong to the same tree, and if so, where. The more you trust the process of discovery, better. Keep working, and if it feels right, it will probably fit.

Devoted to Flow

As freewriters in the flow, it becomes important to engage our writing at the visceral level, and we do this primarily because it fuels us. It vitalizes our process. Being in touch with the visceral doesn't mean all your writing always needs to be bursting at the seams with description like a romantic thriller. The gift of viscerally-fueled writing is that it can bring into your voice the signature of spontaneity. Freshness.

When you are in touch with your own viscerality, you don't need to ask anyone's permission before you write something. You don't feel the need to ask your critic "Is this OK? Is it good?" Instead, you can rest on your curiosity for what is happening in the moment.

Rather than believing that we need to gain dominion and control over the imagination by analyzing it, we can simply rest where we are, engaged with the vulnerable spontaneous present moment, moving towards authenticity. Anything at all might happen at any moment.

The more fully we abide in the devotional, the more we are able to convey inspirational force, the better we can rest, relax, and afford to have confidence that what we need will be supplied in the moment it's called for. Even when we do not get what we ask for, it is immensely better to be surprised by writing that has real vitality.

The imagination is superior to the mind. When we try and control the imagination with the mind, we resist the flow of inspiration. Inspiration is our connection with something higher.

So, as you set out on your voyage to do a writing marathon, take heart. Look at it this way: if you let yourself write something really bad, it helps you feel better about all the other stuff you merely find questionable.

As freewriters we experience ourselves to be big enough to make mistakes and sensitive enough to perceive them and nimble enough to be fueled by them and trusting or confident enough to embrace it all.

Bag of Tricks

Here are a few reminders of some things to keep in your bag of tricks as you freewrite.

Make Metaphors

If you feel stuck, make strings of metaphors. Use "like" or "as" to make connection after connection. Stretch your analogies as far as you want.

Change Registers

When you feel like making a shift but don't necessarily know what you want to write about, change registers. Write more viscerally or cerebrally, or a different voice or character. Imitate another author. The invitation here is to focus on the way of speaking rather than the things you say.

Get Altitude

As needed, pop upward to a higher elevation view. Give yourself some more choices for where to take things. If you're in the middle of a chapter, you can make lists of possible branches you might want to continue with.

Repeat or Recap

When you're really stuck and you want to keep your focus tight, simply repeat yourself. Circle back and recall what you just wrote, recapping the paragraph, or sentence, or chapter. You can even just repeat the last word you wrote.

Associate

Use the last word or phrase as a jumping-off point for free association. Write the first thing that emerges. Do this again and again until something shifts.

Share a Block / Share a Love

If you feel uninspired or frustrated or blocked, don't turn away from the emotions that arise there. Take it as an opportunity to turn towards them, really feel them, and write about what is coming up for you. Write about your block. Describe it thoroughly and completely with painstakingly high detail.

- Do you feel stuck?
- Do you feel inauthentic?
- Are you not good enough in some way?
- Are you lacking command or authority?
- Are you dependent on the right mood?
- Are you judging your cliches or lifeless language?
- Are you hard on your ability to finish a project?

Describing the problem completely, the solution might even write itself.

Another exercise for the bag of tricks is the "Turning a Phrase" exercise described next.

Turning A Phrase Exercise

One of the challenges with writing is when you have the feeling that things could be said better yet you can't quite see an opening. The writing feels locked down. It becomes hard to discern how they could be said any better.

Maybe you feel like "Well, I said it, and there's nothing more I know how to say about it." Saying it again would only be to repeat yourself.

This exercise helps demonstrate how much it matters the way something gets written. It's not as if you can write something in two different ways and it won't make a difference. The way something gets written is everything.

It can prove a useful exercise to experiment with rapidly restating the same thing in different ways.

1. Bring your attention to the way things get said. Notice the parts, the elements, and the causes of the effects. Notice the verbs and pronouns, whether they are abstract or concrete, experiment with techniques like repetition, turns, shifts of beginning and ending.
2. And then write something.
3. And then write it again a different way.

You're giving yourself options and you're also seeing other sides to the simple thing you wrote in the first place.

For an example, I'll start with a simple sentence:

A man walks down the street.

The phrase might be taken as it is, literally, or it could be received as an image or symbol. Perhaps we see this image as a metaphor for life as well. It resonates with us in that way. And, in a small way, we wonder who the man is, where he came from, where he's going, whether what he carries with him is helping him along.

We can also look at the shape of the thought and think of it poetically in that way. As a shaped thought, it's pretty straightforward; plainly spoken. It's functioning in language in as about a fundamental way as it can. This language is also going somewhere — it does not expect us to slow down and examine the way that the phrase has been laid out.

Going, going, going, the man on the street.

The phrase begins with action — action absent a subject. It takes itself as the subject for the time-being, and we suspend comprehension of all else. The action of going is mixed with the word's repetition, and when we at last come to the man on the street, his figure is mixed in — it's his whirlwind of action.

That man and his walk!

Here we sense the individuation of the man against other potential men potentially walking. The speaker is remarking about a particular man, and in the remark we get a sense of the speaker's individuation as well. We wonder who this person is that he or she reacts in such a way to the walking man. I'm not really changing the information so much as playing with the free space offered by language. It's there; we don't often see how much wiggle room there truly is, because most of the time we seek to convey meaning with the shapes of our thoughts. We are simply getting from point A to point Z.

Once, there was a man who walked down the street.

I love the way this phrasing signifies the beginning of a tale. From thin air, a claim is conjured: Once, such-and-such happened. Once, so-and-so existed. There's something about the removal of the word Once that makes its claim so different than, for example, simply mentioning it: A man walked down the street. The words invite the reader to imagine a parallel space, perhaps in the past — and certainly again in this moment of retelling.

The street had a man walking down it.

Here, the focus is on the street. The man is really just a passing thing, and what's significant is the street, or perhaps the fact that a man was walking on it. Maybe it is a dead-end street, or a street where only women walk.

A man walks uphill down the street.

This sentence shows something peculiar in the telling. It draws our attention to the man and his actions, but primarily we're hung up on why it was phrased that way. This kind of play had better pay off for the reader, because it takes work that distracts us from the feeling that we're going somewhere.

It was a man that walked down the street.

This could be a factual interpretation of the street scene. Just prior to this statement, something must have happened that called into question the gender or manliness of the figure on the street. I'm inclined to read into this phrase beyond the literal distinction from man/not-man and ascribe to the man a kind of Dirty Harry swagger.

Compare it to a similarly constructed sentence:

It was a street that the man was walking on.

Here the speaker is creating the possibility that men can walk on many things: airplane wings, chairs, blades of grass.

Well, a man is walking down the street, after all.

Here we get an image of the world in which the street and the man live. The speaker seems reluctant or dubious about someone walking down the street. Was it too dark? Dangerous? Is the speaker concerned that he/she is alone? Was a house robbed? Why is the speaker seemingly relieved to notice something so commonplace?

It's just a man walking down the street.

Here's a phrase we too often imply internally when we're searching for ideas. We're saying that it's nothing more. As a statement, of course, it's fine, it serves a purpose, it keeps our attention earthbound.

Let's see what happens when drawing attention to this language. A good way to draw more attention to something as writers is to spend more time with it in writing, consciously returning to the insistent word "just" whenever possible:

It's just a man walking down the street. He's just walking. He's doing what you'd expect, and not doing anything besides going down the street. He's just a normal man. It's just a normal street. People walk on streets. This man is doing just that.

When I write resolutely this way, as a writer, I'm inclined to see the insistence as a kind of pressure cooker. I'm inclined to say what is not happening:

It's not like he's stolen your wallet. He's just walking like anyone else would walk. He's not a stuffed dummy; he's walking down the street. Go ahead and look if you don't believe me. See, it's just a man – it's not a whole parade of people even though you keep saying it sounds like that.

There are many potential avenues to explore. I risk expressing that I'm uncertain — and that doubt makes me uncomfortable. The more I learn that it's OK to play with ideas, the more at ease I become with being uncertain. It's about prioritizing the shape of thoughts over the words that are used to form them. As a performance, this writing may take a bit of time to arrive at the crystalline shape that does justice to my interaction.

How to Outmaneuver Stuckness

With freewriting, you really can trust the process. If you commit to writing continually, then you can be assured you will continually write. You can be assured of producing something, and at least some parts of that will be better than other parts. It's natural that quality and coherence and topic will vary. What you produce won't be monolithically locked in place. Therefore, there will always be some elements you can bring forward and refine.

When I write that the process can be trusted, I really mean that. No matter how you feel or what is coming up for you or even if you don't feel like writing, you can potentially benefit from freewriting by simply letting what is actually present be a part of the process for you. If you're happy, let yourself be happy. If you are confused, don't deny the fact that you feel confused. And if you feel stuck, continue to engage the process while allowing your stuck-ness to be present with you.

Essentially, I mean this: don't deny your feelings, thoughts or ideas. And don't let them run the show, either.

Let's take a common example to illustrate this. What happens when you commit to freewriting and then as you're writing you discover that you aren't in the mood? Should you continue? If you freewrite when you aren't in the mood, part of you might try and make the process miserable so that you will feel even more discouraged from trying to freewrite again in the future. In other words, either denying a feeling or allowing it to run the show can be a way of sabotaging yourself. If you persist with writing, trying to smile and tell yourself how happy you are, despite feeling blank and frustrated, it might be a long and annoying voyage.

A small shift makes all the difference. If you persist with the process regardless of your mood, and you simply remain present with how you feel, you will eventually burn away the emotionality that doesn't help you get where you want to go. "I'm not feeling it" becomes "I am not feeling it as much as I want to" which becomes "I love to feel in the flow." By being patient with yourself and trusting your foundational motives, you are able to be productive and to come to a greater understanding of your inner depths.

If you feel stuck, things will eventually improve. But how long is that "eventually?" The more practice you get with freewriting, the less energy you feed stuckness.

There are varying styles and degrees of stuckness. The main thing is to continue to engage no matter what. This is so important. Simple, but of absolute importance.

If you give up, you're giving in to stuckness, allowing it to have the final say as to what you believe yourself to be capable of. When things get especially miserable, you might just decide to quit and walk away. Your experience of freewriting, then, would sum up as a fruitless battle. You'd say "to hell with this, I'll try something that doesn't hurt as much." The problem with doing this is that it chalks up to a loss for your willpower and even your sense of self. I don't mean to sound overly dramatic, though I do feel the need to emphasize this point. When you commit to going with the flow, go with it and keep going with it. Follow through with your agreement and keep giving yourself ongoing minor successes. They may not always feel the best, but they do add up to greater and greater successes over the long run.

It makes it all so much easier if you not only commit to following through with writing without stopping, but also if you give your energy towards strategies that keep you moving in the direction you intended to go (even if that direction is completely open-ended). If you don't make small pivots when you find yourself in negative and sticky spaces, things are apt to just magnify that sticky stuckness.

Something like the example below is common to see:

> I don't know what I'm writign, I'm just writing this instead of actually writign what I want. Here I am again, typing useless words on the page that aren't going to see publishing, and I'm wasting my time. Why would I do this to myself? I must be some sort of glutton for punishment. A punishment glutton. I'm totally indulging thi sside of myself. It's sick. That's what it is. It's sick and I just keep doing it. Ah, if only I had a good idea, I really should sit and wait and then I can come up with something something something. How am I supposed to come up with any ideas when all that I'm doing is talking to myself? I sound like a crazy person. I hope nobody actually reads this. They'll see what rubbish it really is. I don't know who I think I am calling myself a writer. ... and so forth.

We can do better than that.

A few simple tools help to maneuver yourself out of an emotional funk. As with the "bag of tricks" that helps when you feel like writing but don't seem to have any workable ideas, it's important to remember that there is tremendous value in allowing yourself to presence your feelings and be real with how you really feel at any given moment. If you're angry, allow the anger to be there. If you're depressed, allow the sadness. At the moment, it's just you and the page. There really is no sense in forcing away any feelings. The philosophy here is to be real and to write with a sense of presence.

By the same token, this isn't an invitation to wallow in emotions or allow them to lead you around in circles and convolutions. The central aim is to feel yourself substantial enough to remain in touch with your innermost desire to write despite whatever the other factors are. The fact of the matter is that you have something you want to write, somewhere you want to go. So these strategies are offered as a way to help you get there.

Switch what criticism carries

This strategy gets you to use the impulse for judgment but not its content. The desire to criticize or judge can be powerful. We can use that to our advantage if we decouple the judgment from what it wants to claim. Think of it as slyly switching identical briefcases with someone.

Self-criticism does not belong in a freewriting session. The same is true of judgment. Nevertheless, judgment and self-criticism probably will want to pop in and say something. The rules don't permit you to listen to content of their impulse to speak. However, you can use the force of impulse to speak.

Have you ever noticed the sharpness and insistence that often comes with criticism? If you're feeling boggy or uninspired, that impulse can bring remarkable clarity and directness. Even if that sharpness only has something like "Well, I suck" to offer you. It really can cut through a hazy space.

Think of criticism as a horse carrying a wagon of negative judgment. Your job is to be a sneaky ninja and decouple the horse from the negative wagon and hitch it to a creative wagon. The horse is strong and its new creative wagon is full of all sorts of life and vibrancy.

What does this look like in practice? Well, it's a subtle shift.

At times, you may suspect that what you're writing might be utter garbage. This suspicion doesn't feel good. You've been at it for twenty minutes and it feels like torture. The earthquakes of inner turmoil may eventually rouse the beast of criticism currently chained to the dungeon floor.

All seems eerily silent, the air pregnant with foreboding. You have the sense of something terrible in the distance. The scent of stuckness pervades your space. It's all too much.

At last, the beast wakes.

The beast of stuckness is a real jerk. It only wants to say bad things about you and your project.

"You're no good." "All you write is garbage." "You're stuck because you are a lousy writer."

And so forth. Everyone already knows what the beast is going to say. It's no surprise that the beast of stuckness is very unoriginal.

Based on this, we tend to assume that our inner beast of stuckness only wants bad things for us. That we should somehow slay the beast and be free of the weight of a terrible critic. That's not what I want to suggest.

The problem with the beast of stuckness is precisely that it doesn't know what to say. It has a boring script that it simply repeats. So, the strategy to take here is to give it a better script. By doing this, you can begin to transform the beast into a helpful ally. All you have to do is change its script from the default negative criticism to something else.

To do this, your job is to catch the impulse. Instead of only hearing what it says, learn to notice the signs of its presence. Maybe its critical voice has a characteristic flavor or texture in your psyche. Don't accept what it says as if it is true. Don't let the beast of stuckness speak using your voice. With practice, you begin to notice it as distinct from your inner drive to create. Your voice is different from that of the beast. In the beginning it can be hard to discern this – we believe the negative things we hear are our own beliefs, statements of truth assessing our writing. Not so. These beliefs belong to the beast of stuckness.

Fortunately, you can give the beast something better to do with its energy. You can replace the old tired usual criticism with a few empowering questions. That way, the next time you feel stuck and the monster wakes, it will ask you for pointers as to how you can more fully engage the flow.

The inner critic doesn't know what to say. Give it the opportunity to chime in with critically engaging questions installed there by the creative impulse. Eventually, instead of stopping when you feel stuck, you can use the critical positioning of consciousness to deepen your engagement. Instead of saying "You're having trouble writing because you're a lousy writer," the critical monster can ask you "What am I most drawn to in this?"

It's sweet, really. And like that, your creative impulse has a bit more fuel. It has been shocked out of the fog. Disrupted towards clarity.

It's all thanks to some subtle behind-the-scenes shifts.

It's possible that none of this will actually be revealed in the text of your writing. In your freewritten material, there might just be a slew of flat junk, and then suddenly it shifts.

You decided "Enough with this shit, I'm going to focus on what I want, not sit here and complain to myself."

Like magic, an idea comes to you and you start producing solid gold brilliance.

It might look something like this:

... They'll see what rubbish it really is. I don't know who I think I am calling myself a writer. I really should sit and wait and then I can come up with something. How am I supposed to come up with any ideas when all that I'm doing is talking to myself? I sound like a crazy person. I hope nobody actually reads this. They'll see what rubbish it really is. I don't know who I think I am calling myself a writer. Gerald sat down his whiskey glass and looked into her eyes. "This is the last time you call me that name." The greyhound bus made a low rumble as it accelerated. etc.

Just pretend that's actually solid gold, and you'll see what I mean. You can see that there's a contrast there from the negative self-talk to something in-scene that clicks into focus.

It's like suddenly a switch gets flipped, and you're back in the game.

To do this, simply hold the intention to be discerning about your inner voice. Watch for signs that the beast of stuckness is near, ready to recite the old familiar lines that would stop inspiration from flowing freely.

Patience and persistence goes a long way here. When you find yourself stuck in judgment, try sticking with the process, trusting your foundational intent to create. Feel, feel, feel your way forward. Honestly, it can feel like you're in a dark room reaching for the lightswitch. You knock over everything on the table, scrape your hand across something sharp, hit your head on the wall, then lo! there's the switch. You flip it, and like magic, you can proceed with life as a civilized person again.

When you're aware that you really want to work on your story, when you've had enough, things will work themselves out. If you feel yourself lapsing into flatness where your creative impulse feels tortured by the dreams of the critical giant, you don't need to overpower him. Let him be roused and deliver you a message: an empowering question to reposition your awareness.

Getting Unstuck

When you feel stuck, talk about what you want, not what you don't want.

It's fine to complain. At times, it can even work like rocket fuel for your process. Just don't get stuck in the way that complaints view the world or otherwise you will begin to see everything through the lens of what you don't want and what's wrong about everything. Be with the vitality of them for as long as those feelings are present to you.

So, periodically check in by asking yourself centering questions. Make a simple pivot towards the positive, even if it feels remote. Instead of judging, criticizing, and complaining, and generally bringing on the negative, focus on what you do want. Even if it feels impossible, it's always possible for you to at least be willing to looking in that direction. What you do want – in your life generally, and specifically with regard to this project?

Shifting stance is a much better option than stopping. It stinks to stop and walk away from your writing while you're in the middle of a negative space. It feels like you're getting away from it, but that dark cloud will follow you.

Stuckness's Tripline

There are many ways that a person can play games on themselves, and this is one of them: "Oh, I've hit a snag, so I should stop and think this through."

If you do stop, don't think things through. If you stop, then really take a break. Get some fresh air, move, and change mental channels. Do something brief and honest-to-God restorative. Lay down for five minutes. It's miraculous what can happen when you let yourself do that, be blank, and let the quiet chaos of being horizontal work its magic on you. Especially if you really give yourself total permission to enjoy it because you trust that you will return to writing after five minutes.

Reference Something From Before and Use That As a Branch Forward

The idea here is to feel back into the flow. Not to recreate it or improve upon it necessarily, just to feel back into it and see what happens as you trace it forward. This can be a scene, an idea, anything that was sort of working. Even a "maybe" can lead to something that in the end is totally workable. A lousy idea is better than no idea because it has been made manifest. Let it be what it is, and move forward from it. Nothing about your piece is set in stone yet. Your perspective isn't omniscient. What feels like a bad idea in the moment might turn out all right. Maybe it only looked bad because you were in a foul mood.

Change Something Completely Unrelated to Your Writing

Move to a different location. Elevate your legs. Write with your eyes closed. Hum nonsense to yourself. Speak what you're writing out loud in a funny voice.

You get the idea.

Adjust Your Posture

Have you heard about those studies that have proven the ways that our physiology influences our state of being? The studies show that if you hold a certain posture for a couple of minutes, you tend to gravitate towards the emotional state conveyed by that posture. If you stand up, raise your hands out to the side, and grin from ear to ear, it's impossible to feel as depressed as if you were sitting slumped forward in your chair. The reverse is also true: if you sit slumped forward in your chair, it's hard to feel hugely expansive and confident.

Take a Physicality Break

When you're frustrated, move. When you've totally lost your steam, move. When you're going, going, going in the middle of a freewriting session, going, going, going at it, you tend to space out (or is it space in?) and even forget that you have a physical body.

However, you do actually have a physical body. It has a lot to offer your ability to write. For fifteen minutes, breathe deeply. Move and stretch. Be in nature. Drink deeply of the beauty of outdoors. Chat with a neighbor.

Do something physical rather than stare at another screen for a few minutes.

Handwriting versus Typing

Which should you do? Your preference here. There's no right answer. Nothing substitutes the texture and organic richness of handwriting.

I tend to believe that typing is more of a time-saver, since you can cut, copy, paste and reorder so easily. Yet, some things can be done on the page that just can't happen on the computer. Drawing arrows, skipping around and flipping through pages. Meandering and merging lines. There's no substitute to the advanced technology that is handwriting on paper. However, if you have a good relationship with your computer, if typing feels organic to you, then by all means. Go with it. It's what I do most of the time.

Particularly if you're pressed for time, one might make the case for typing. But don't feel pressured into typing if you don't find it organic. Better to go with the flow than against it.

Bringing Order

Trust the Wider Order of the Imagination

Deep freewriting is more than just a simple exercise. It's a journey. You're doing something unique, engaging something bigger than the ordinary mind when you freewrite. Yes, it's chaotic at times. But honor the imagination and you can expect to be more productive and more fluid about the creative process.

First Life, Then Shape

When you write, and especially when you freewrite, things don't need to come out in perfect order. The main thing is that they come out. As overwhelming as it may seem at times, it's much easier to organize messy writing than it is to try to organize writing before a word of it has been written.

Another thing to remember is that there is no single right way or best order to impose on your writing. There are no limits to how you can make freewriting work for you. You can freewrite a novel. You can freewrite a grocery list. You can freewrite to help get a sense of clarity about the right order of a complex task. Later, you can move right into a different activity like mind mapping, either referencing what you write, or just regarding the freewriting as an exercise that churns up ideas from the chaos.

Freewriting this way is like rehearsing for the next step. Maybe you're writing a letter to an old friend and you don't know how you want to start it. The direct path, diving right in with a freewrite that you intend to reorder and revise, can give you the needed clarity.

Here are some techniques for improving the organization and structural clarity of a freewriting session.

Use White Space

Freewriting, people fear, produces a bunch of unordered material. What they seem to forget is that nothing requires a freewriter to mash everything into a single paragraph. You can give yourself as much space as you like. It sounds so simple and it is, but the power of blank white space can be profoundly helpful. Space between paragraphs indicates a separation of thoughts or a change of gears. It's an effortless thing you can do to make things easier for yourself later when you read back through your writing.

#Label Your Text (As Needed)

Also, feel free to label things as they occur to you. Put notes to yourself in quotes or use hashtags. Whatever works to make separate parts that signify something. Mark the text in the moment. Leave any and all notes to yourself right there in the text.

The important thing is to experiment with all sorts of methods with the understanding that you only need to adopt what feels like a good fit for you. The more you use a method that works for you, the more you internalize the benefits of it, the more you are able to simply show up to the page and start writing. This has definitely been the case for me.

I remember going through phases when I would labor over every word, sit and scrape out the words like every one was the last bit of something at the bottom of a jar. It was only after I had done a great deal more writing, and freewriting specifically, that I formed a solid relationship with the written word. Now when I write, the only real delay for me beginning is to get familiar with the project I'm working on, and whether that means reading a bit that comes before, or looking at the outline, or doing a bit of sketching-writing. Then I begin, and I can keep at it until I feel like stopping or it's done.

Having the sense of a destination helps tremendously Most of the time spent writing is time spent not writing – sitting there blankly struggling and thinking. The challenges magnify when you don't know where you want to take your writing. On the other hand, when you know what you want to say, whether it's a sentence or a chapter or a whole series of books, saying it can be fairly straightforward.

Don't get me wrong here. If you're writing a novel, this doesn't necessarily mean that you need to know how your book ends, or that the fast way of writing is also the way that spoils the mystery.

It's true that one of the most significant factors with a slow writing output has to do with knowing where you're going. Though, you don't actually need to know everything about where you intend to go.

In my experience, the main way to make this work is to have in mind some key points or nodes that you'll want to move towards. Really, even having a single point can be enough to get the juices flowing. What most often happens is that you get going and before long, you have more ideas than you need, and it's a matter of being strategic and keeping a general workmanlike pace. No need to rush unless you really want to.

The model to visualize here is that of the tree. Your topic is your tree, so you need a clear sense of the tree's trunk, which translates to the main topic you're bringing to your reader. Coming from that main topic are only a few really large branches. Those are your most important elements, the ones you know the best. From there comes all the other branches and leaves. What the reader sees is the enormous complex tree in its wholeness - leaves, limbs – it's alive. To you, you feel the tree, and you have a thorough sense for the tree from the tree's perspective. You know your story like you know yourself because you are inside it, embodying it, exploring it.

The beautiful thing about when you work according to this model is that you can be completely trusting of inspiration. If you need to, you can write in any order, because you basically know where everything goes. Anything that comes to you can be honored and find its place. No need to follow all the correct prescriptions for how to write, because you know your project better than anyone. It belongs to you, and you don't need to struggle to find ideas. They come to you.

To make the tree model work for you, you'll need to give some consideration for the context of your project and leave yourself space for the details until they actually occur to you. You might see your freewriting like a kind of scanning of the space around the tree, where the act of freewriting brings you these ongoing distinctions – this is the tree, this is just the air between the limbs, and that belongs to some other plant. The more you explore in your freewriting, the more you get a holographic sense of the tree that is your project.

Through trial and error, you become nimble with what belongs to the project and what doesn't. Drafting it is much easier when you have this sense, just like it's easier to have an in-depth and intimate conversation with someone you know very well versus someone with whom you have no rapport.

Different Altitudes, Different Levels of Perspective

Outlining is higher-altitude - more broad in scope, and without much resolution regarding specifics. Drafting is low-elevation. It's on-the-ground traversal of the terrain. Intimate, descriptive, lived-in. Without much perspective about the broad scope. Hard to navigate from Texas to Manhattan when looking at the world only through a magnifying glass. Easy when looking down at a map; there's less to take in.

Leave White Space

When you're freewriting, things occur to you at different levels. You may be hiking the terrain and some really key plot points occur to you. What should you do? Hold them in mind? Tuck them away somewhere? True to the practice, you can simply put them down as you flow forward at your regular pace. A simple strategy for making this work is to press return a couple of times before and after this bit of text. Give yourself a bit of white space and then continue forward, either with material within that point or continuing to chart forward.

Leave Notes

Just like how things occur at different elevations, things also occur for you at different registers. What do I mean by register? Think of registers as different voices that you take as you write. One is an announcer voice, another is a character's voice. Another is the narrator voice. One voice belongs to a different project. Another register might be some aspect of stuckness or writer's block speaking through you. Recognizing the register can help you know how to navigate what is being said.

Don't worry, though, if it's not always clear to you what the voice belongs to. There's no requirement to know everything or to be able to label every section. Generally, the longer you work on a project, the more lived-in it feels, and the easier it becomes to discern between the different registers within that project.

As with other comments and notes to yourself, label the registers of different sections as it occurs to you, whether before or after the fact. If you write a paragraph and want to give a title to that paragraph, then write the title when it occurs to you and keep going from there. Better to stay in the flow than to start jumping around the document.

Sometimes when I am writing and I don't feel called to finish one section, I'll put down a list of how I want to break it down, with the understanding that I can come back to do that at some later point. I'll leave the list undeveloped and move on to whatever else happens to be alive for me in the moment. It's a pretty safe move, since I know that once I have a list, I have some structure to rest on there. I can come back to it later and feel my way back into it as an outline for more ideas.

A list is a great tool to use during freewriting. Just because you're in the flow of ideas doesn't mean you are stuck in a given flow of language or paragraph structure. The singular rule is to keep writing. It's not a complex rule. It means that you do not stop writing, which also means you don't divert yourself by looking back through what you've written yet. So yes, write without stopping. Though, just as when talking, you can change your tone or move around, the same is true for freewriting. You can change modes, skip forward, change modalities.

Modalities include:

- Writing what you intend to write
- Sketching
- Listing
- Talking to yourself through your writing
- Exploring your purpose
- Writing to feel the qualities of your audience
- Questioning about your desired outcome

- Being with and expressing what you're feeling as a means to get beneath your feelings

Organizing As You Go

As mentioned, labeling or #commenting / tagging sections can be done on-the-fly. It's easy, lightweight, fast. There's no reason not to do this. It allows you to refer back to some part more easily so that later when you reread and revise, you can get more of a sense for how to reorder things. Trust me, in the flow, you'll be awake to things that may not be as obvious to you later when you are rereading things. This happens when ideas are really flooding you faster that you can render them in words. Meta-writing like comments gives you an anchor which you can reference if the same vein returns to you later in your freewrite.

For me, it can look like this:

> Something something something something something something something #topic6 something something ... (32 more lines of this) Something something #topic2 something

In that example, you can see how I left some organizational comments for myself. Rereading back through this, I can easily realize that I intended to group the two items together. In no time, I can reorder things. Even though it looks like a big monolithic tangle, it's actually trivial to make well-ordered.

Strategic use of whitespace. For whatever reason, you want to set some stuff apart. This is great for avoiding the scary monolithic paragraph of intense freewriting.

If you're writing by hand, you can also effortlessly do things like draw lines or shapes that key your revising-self in on what you're up to.

A trail of breadcrumbs shows the way back home. Breadcrumbing is a special form of commenting where your comments are descriptive of the hierarchy or order of the project. A natural way of employing this is if you have chapters, then headers and subheaders. If you write things out of order, you can simply add a comment near the section indicating where within the project it belongs.

> Something something something something something something something #chapter7/mainsection something something
>
> Something something something something something something something
>
> ... (32 more lines of this)
>
> Something something #chapter44/conclusion something something ...
>
> Something something something something something something something

The comments with the slash indicate where these parts fit in the order of things.

As you can see, even a little can go a long way when it comes to organizing while freewriting. Nothing needs to be properly formatted or ornate. A few jots, a light bit of notation here and there, can make all the difference when it comes time to reread what you wrote.

Strategies for Making the Most of Your Writing Marathon

To make the most of your writing marathon, it's beneficial to have in mind an overarching vision for the endeavor.

As with anything done punctually or as a ritual, it can be powerful to avail yourself before you begin the ritual of setting a conscious intention and welcoming something relevant to a specific question or goal.

Exploring Your Beliefs and Emotions

You might want to do a writing marathon to gain mastery or clarity about some limiting belief that keeps you blocked. It's very likely, depending on how long your marathon lasts, that you will experience some ups and downs.

Limiting beliefs keep us in pain, in mediocrity, in self-sabotage. Limiting beliefs are at the root of what keep writers locked and blocked and frustrated.

Breakthroughs do not need to be an uncommon thing. Breakthroughs, even big ones, can happen all the time. There are no limits here.

The Physicality Aspect of Writing for Long Durations

Is a writing marathon exhausting?

In my experience, fatigue comes from the strain of doing something. In my experience, strain seems to be an added layer of suffering that layers on top of the actual effort required to do something. Broadly speaking, it's unnecessary and actually counterproductive. There's nothing that says if you write without stopping for two hours you'll be exhausted and drained afterward. I have found the opposite to be true.

When you decide to write nonstop for a long period of time, you basically decide to gear into the endeavor without straining, since that would lead to undue exhaustion. When a writing marathon is going well, it feels nourishing. When your writing drains you, you're doing something wrong. Either you're fighting with yourself, or you're straining to make things better than they are, or you are generally just doing something that places undue constraints on yourself.

You can sit and watch a marathon of TV shows and movies, sometimes for hours at a time, and follow plotlines and the emotional stress of other peoples creation. Why should it be different if you are the one doing the creating?

Writing does have a physical component, and it's not to be disregarded. RSI, repetitive strain injuries, carpal tunnel, and many other health concerns can play a part in your writing life. Hands get strained from moving a pen for hours. Fingers and forearms get fatigued and tight or even numb from typing for hours on end. Bodies become stiff, backs exhausted, spines out of alignment. Eyes get tired. Brains get bleary. Being sedentary can be terrible for your health.

But what I have noticed is that people will justify or even totally ignore the strain when it's for other activities yet complain about it when it's due to writing for long stretches. People will disagree with writing only to go exhaust themselves by playing video games for hours at a time or staring at a tablet or slaving away at horrible office work where you are required to perform, yet because it's someone else requiring it of you, and because you need that paycheck, you justify the strain of it.

Why not push yourself at least as much as you allow others to push you?

Here are some lethal doses of motivation and strategy to destroy your limiting beliefs and excuses, the barriers that hold you back from manifesting your heart's desire.

Make Your Breaks Rejuvenating

In short, take breaks... and make good use of your breaks

You're sitting at your desk writing for two hours straight. Your timer goes off. You get up and go outside. Breathe deeply. Start walking. If you feel like it, go for a brief jog. Do a round of energizing breathwork. Do a short sequence of hatha yoga postures. Play with your dog. Go for a brief swim. Talk to other human beings. Then when your fifteen minutes is up, come back inside and park yourself at your writing desk and resume the pleasure of working.

Don't: Just lay down or stay seated there. Your break is your opportunity to introduce some fresh energy into your system. It's important to move, to change scenery, give yourself real energetic support. Not just a break from the task, but real rejuvenation.

Stand up while writing

There was a stand-up desk craze a few years back, and eventually after hearing about it enough I was willing to try it out. It helped me be more productive because of the simple fact that instead of slouching in my chair I was standing there. My body was telling me, "Hey, you're standing up. There is a job to do. Stay focused." It wasn't fatiguing.

I don't know that it was a miraculous answer or that all the reputed health benefits of a standing desk are bonafide, but I support it as a worthwhile addition to your productivity pallette. When I did my 24 hour writing marathon, I spent about half the time standing. I could move my feet or fidget as I needed. It was helpful to do this during the latter half of the marathon, when things got a little weird just from general fatigue and entering a bit of an altered state.

Maybe it's hard to explain just why, but standing while writing was especially pivotal when my physical energy level waned. It helped me stay active and in the flow. So even if you prefer to write while seated in a desk or on your bed or at a coffee shop, I want to be emphatic about the benefit of writing while standing at least part of the time during your marathon.

Write Using Dictation

The same awkwardness that faces you when you are new to freewriting is there when you start out with voice dictation. If you're like me, you feel xenophobic when being recorded, like there is all this silence that needs to be filled with your speech. Instead of only the blank page staring at you, the whole room is waiting for you to say something. All your vocal missteps seem to be magnified. All the ums, uhs, and tangled sentence structure are embarrassing.

Yes, yes... except... You are freewriting! You are making forward momentum, and all without lifting a finger! What a miracle this is!

How to make voice dictation work for you? Basically, just be patient with yourself to get into the flow. The words come out, and they are usable, and you can just pace around the room and spout verbal brilliance. Your magic invisible assistant is hanging on every word.

And, if you are using transcription software, every word is dutifully shape-changed into physical words on the screen. Gone are the physical constraints of the pen or the keyboard. No longer are you tethered to any specific workstation. You can use your smartphone or a wireless headset to record your audio as you pace and meander and wave your hands in the air, gesticulating to your imagined reader.

As with writing while standing, voice dictation is definitely worth trying. Not only is it very efficient (in its way), but you also tap into a different modality: speech. You're no longer working with letters and symbols but syllables and phonemes. You can connect your viscerality to your engagement with the written word, actively feeling in your vocal cords the textures of your language.

You tap into a new and interesting rhythm, and ideas will land for you somewhat differently than when writing by hand or on the keyboard. For some, speaking aloud is helpful because they can better sense that they are connecting with an audience. As when explaining something out loud to a friend, we make our language clear and direct.

If you're feeling stuck with a writing project, give yourself the opportunity to bypass your blocks by talking yourself through it. Adhere to the same constant forward momentum as when freewriting. In a way, it may be easier to do this, to disregard what you just said, because there won't be the physical representation of your words on the screen (unless you're using dictation software and actively torturing yourself with its on-screen display). You can just flow and flow, and let the forward momentum help you refine your intent.

One of the opportunities that makes voice transcription a real gem is how you can write while doing other things. Need to load the dishwasher and prep tomorrow's casserole? No problem— you can stack these activities together and do them while you freewrite. Right there in your kitchen, you can pen your bestseller. Just tell anyone within earshot that they might want to ignore the imaginary conversation you're having.

There are lots of good options for how you want to do your voice freewriting. If you have a smartphone, you can find an app – most likely even a free one – that records audio. Many apps can transcribe the audio as well.

It won't be perfect, but we're freewriting, so we aren't bothered by a lack of perfection. It happens all the time that what seems like a mistake is actually an opportunity. Have you ever had autocorrect give you a suggestion that wasn't what you intended? Sometimes these are absurd, and often they are funny. Sometimes, though different, they are better than what you had in mind. The same can be true with dictation mistakes. Have fun with it, and see what happens.

When in doubt, you can relisten to the audio file to be sure. As long as you have a clear vision for your project, you'll know what to do when an uncertainty arises. Such chaos and weirdness can work wonders for stirring up new developments with your writing style and your project's voice.

Tip: Look for an audio recorder with VAR, the voice-activated recording feature. This is a huge time saver if you tend to go for spans of time without saying anything. When you are silent, the recorder pauses. It resumes when you begin talking. Whether you take a few seconds or a few minutes, the recorder doesn't mind. It will wait patiently for you until you speak. Some handheld voice recorders can do this. Audacity is a free computer application with this feature.

Reclining Desk

Oh, you read that right. Yes, there are desks made for the express purpose of writing while either laying back in a chair or in bed. Don't tell me that doesn't sound awesome.

Over the years, I have experimented with all sorts of different ways of writing. This one, when I heard about it, had an instant appeal.

Combine this with voice transcription and you might feel like you're laying on Freud's couch. That sounds like something to try, yeah?

Though, for me, despite my excitement for it, I found this method harder than expected.

When I lay on my back, I felt like I was tapping into some very spacious daydreamy sort of qualities. Just by orienting my body differently, I was accessing a very different state-specific way of thinking and feeling. The trouble was... I found it hard to stay productive. It was relaxing. I found it hard to stay on point, focused, and motivated. It would have been better for doing something passive, rather than active.

But give it a try! Anything can happen.

Write While On the Road

To be clear, unless you're doing voice transcription, writing while driving is not a good idea.

Something engages when we are traveling in a car or on a plane. We feel forward momentum and an exciting sense of being rooted and at the same time dynamically uprooted. Unless you get carsick. Then again, voice transcription can come to the rescue.

Riding on trains can be marvelous for this as well. The gentle vibration, background murmur, and occasional swaying or rocking has a real charm.

Write While Listening to Music

Loud music, soft music, try it all. Also, if you want, you can experiment with actively engaging the music rather than just having it be there as wallpaper to your experience. Write with awareness of timbre, rhythm, and the general atmosphere of the music. Let it come through in your writing. It can be hard to write to music that has vocals, but this can also be an interesting challenge to pose to yourself, specifically if you are writing music. I have had some really great experiences writing lyrics while listening to other music. The music was loud. I didn't use any of the same words, and my lyrics weren't made to fit with the stuff I was listening to. I just used the music as a device to pummel against my consciousness to get me to feel like I was in the hot seat. Those rough-draft lyrics worked just fine. I changed a few things. It may be true that some of the best song lyrics were never really fussed over, but composed pretty much spontaneously.

Write While Walking

Walk a path and write as you do so. Later, retrod the same path and add more material. This sort of exercise can tap into the perks of a "memory mansion" realm of experience.

What is a memory mansion? As I understand it, the technique of the memory mansion dates back to the ancient Greeks. They prized oration, and were very good at memorization. With a memory mansion, first you have a mental map of a specific place – a house, maybe. Then when you want to remember things, you can simply place these objects at different locations of your memory mansion. When you need to remember them, you simply re-trod the path and you can discover what you left there.

My hands-on way to apply this is to go for a walk. As you walk, associate different parts of your book with different areas of your walk. Speak out loud into your voice recorder as you walk. Make mental notes when you come across different landmarks.

You can mention the landmarks or not, depending on what feels right for your project. When you read or listen back through your material, you will probably remember the landmarks of your walk.

Definitely worth trying. See the difference when you make your walk an intentional part of your process.

Alternate Between Modalities

If you will be freewriting for any stretch (say, above two hours), it is a good idea to vary your modalities. In a way, this makes your marathon into a triathlon.

You can do this one of two ways, either deciding beforehand how long you will write in each given way, or allow yourself to switch between them organically. The latter can work only if you set everything up beforehand in such a way that there is no delay.

You want to keep the forward momentum regardless of whether you are transitioning from sitting to standing or standing to voice transcription. If you decide to plan your modalities beforehand, it gives you the opportunity to work on more than one project, if you'd like.

Switching some modalities may not automatically bring about a change in your state of mind, but others may. For me, I often notice a shift when moving between typing and handwriting. But not necessarily any when transitioning from sitting to standing. So if I happen to have more than one project on my plate, I can use this to my advantage. I can use my computer time to flesh out scenes of a novel-in-progress, then my handwriting time to explore future business plans and goals. The space around them is totally different, but the general momentum of creation can be synergistic. Alternatively, I can stick to the same project throughout, and just be curious about what emerges by engaging in the different modalities of language creation.

Example triathlon:

1. 2 hours computer writing seated at my desk
2. 15 minute break: yoga postures and breathwork

3. 1 hour voice transcription
4. 15 minute break: a walk through the neighborhood
5. 1 hour standing writing by hand
6. 1 hour seated writing at computer desk

Since I'm encouraging you to write for heroically long spans, I should also mention a few things you can do to work out the tension and strain from long writing sessions.

Basically any basic stretches can be helpful, paying particular attention to the shoulder complex and forearms.

Simple activities are my favorite. For releasing tension in the wrists and forearms, you can press your forearm down against a rubber ball, foam roller, or tennis ball to work out the tightness in the forearm.

It's also a great exercise to stand in a doorway with your arms spread wide, then gently and slowly lean forward, bringing a stretch to your arm, shoulder and chest.

I have found that nothing beats yoga for working out tightness anywhere in the body. The most fruitful approach is to work and stretch the whole body, not just the areas experiencing tightness or pain. It's all connected.

Any yoga is good. All of your muscle fascia and tendons are connected at least indirectly. You might think that your tight hamstrings have no effect on your back, but stretching your hamstrings might work wonders for neck pain. The same is true for strengthening your upper back because you want to address some tightness in your forearms. Strong upper back muscles aid in good posture. Having good posture helps hugely for everything downstream, which is to say, your upper and lower arms.

Honest to God, even if you just do regular good stretches and go for occasional walks you will be in the top quintile. The way we are collectively learning to treat our bodies is abysmal. Don't do this. Be fantastic. The fundamentals of basic movement and stretching and good posture and oxygenation and having enough variety in your life makes a huge improvement. Don't shortcut yourself. There are no long-term workarounds for this.

Your health is a foundation of your attitude and outlook. It's hard to be truly motivated just from the neck up. You need the support of all your body's systems. That way, you can be fully present and good ideas can consistently land for you.

Be Kind, Be Forgiving

Word count isn't everything. No need to overprioritize sheer content production. If all that mattered was churning out paragraphs, writers could quickly be replaced by artificial intelligence. What AI cannot do is what you yourself are uniquely good at: being yourself. So while it can feel really good to be extremely productive and you feel like you are a content generation machine, it feels even better when you are true to your own voice, generating material that is truly yours. When the ideas and words could only have come from you, then you're really honoring yourself and your long-term trajectory as a writer.

That's yet another benefit of the sketching phase of the freewriting process. During that phase, you can consult with a bigger part of yourself, asking questions and assessing your current project so that it feels aligned with your long-term vision and short-term goals. You don't need to commit yourself to the project before it clicks with you.

It's not objectively better to produce ten times more material if producing that material doesn't bring you more into your depths. So, as you freewrite, be sure that you are checking in with yourself periodically. Small shifts in perspective can end up making a huge long-term impact.

Rules and Regulations

1. Regulation I: (Duration) — Write for the duration, by longhand or on whatever device you'd like.

2. Regulation II: (Rate) — Write/type at the rate of one letter per second or faster. This rate is the required minimum, not a required mean that would be calculated over the entire time period. (Plod; don't write for a burst and then rest.)

3. Regulation III: (Breaks) — Take a fifteen-minute break every three hours. Get up and move around. Then return 100% to your writing.

4. Regulation IV: (Continuity) — Don't look back and reread what was written. Don't be concerned with quality. Do, however, focus on relishing the experience and being fully engaged.

Strategic Pausing

Breaks and pauses can make for more focused and productive writing time. Not allowing yourself any shifts, breaks, pauses, or variety in your writing regime can make it hard to stay focused and motivated. If your mind and body want to take a break but you won't let yourself, you might find yourself blanking out or writing low-quality stuff.

The truth is that most of the time spent "writing" is actually time spent doing something besides writing: thinking trying to come up with ideas to make sense of what you already have written trying to decide what you should say next doing some useless activity to avoid your writing and distract yourself, basically to bleed yourself of time and energy so you no longer have the option of working writing material that won't amount to anything because it isn't good enough, doesn't fit with your project, doesn't make sense, or isn't really something any reader will want to make sense of staring blankly at the wall or out the window. Avoid it by keeping yourself on track: follow your timer and adhere to the work / rest schedule.

Particularly during longer freewriting sessions, it may be advantageous to take a breather. Maybe you want to write for eight solid hours, and you decide you'd like to take a break every two hours for fifteen minutes. On your break you can move around, stretch, or go outside for a breath of fresh air.

After fifteen minutes, you resume, clicking back into gear. When you do this during the creative mode, it's best to stay in the creative mode. And it's definitely good to actually give yourself a break. Resist pouring back through your material. Go for a walk. A run. Lay down for a bit.

Ideally, go for a walk or some restorative physical activity just prior to beginning a freewrite. Then after you're finished with everything, get out there and get physical to release your efforts and celebrate.

Using a Break to Divide creative and critical Modes

A good time for a break is during the natural transition between creative and critical modes.

If you do decide to do a break to split up the creative from the critical mode, it can be really beneficial to read through what you wrote before taking the break. I have found that if I take the break without reading through, it reset things too much, and I lose track of where I was going. Reading back through helps me to hold in mind the main points of what I wrote about.

If the project is really rough, a break basically clears out my short-term memory and when I later read back through, it feels like reading someone else's writing.

Experiment. It's good to reset things, to let go and welcome a fresh flow of vitality in your system.

When you don't feel like doing something energetic like going for a run, it can be very helpful to take a re-centering moment to pause, close your eyes, breathe deeply and fully, and feel the earth beneath you. Pause and ground. Take deep breaths, go inside, and let go of thoughts as much as possible.

The more you allow yourself to really let go, the more you make yourself available to the good ideas that get churned up through the act of freewriting.

What To Do With All Your Freewritten Material?

Each writing session will have a somewhat different flavor. Some days it will be clear what you should do with the stuff that you wrote. Most sessions will produce a mixture of keepers and garbage.

It's useful to have a system of organization that works for you so that if you decide to go back through what you wrote, you can have easy ways of putting the right material in the right place.

Don't Keep Any

The simplest organizational scheme is to regard all your freewriting as stuff to let go of as soon as you write it. It was about the process of writing, not something that anyone, including yourself should ever read. It's an incidental record, nothing more. A flow in a stream that has come and gone, an ephemeral step in an ongoing process. Once written, you read through your material, and proceed from there.

In this scenario, the first pass of freewriting is warmup, to be gotten rid of. There can be some benefit to this method, since it is not always comfortable to be surrounded by thousands and thousands of your own words.

Clutter is not helpful, so you can simply toss all this material right into the trash when you finish.

keep Some, kill the Rest

If you do want to keep some material, the very act of reading back through can be a useful exercise in learning about yourself and knowing where you are at any given phase of the flow. At some points in your freewrite, you may have been refining old ideas. At other points you were drafting new material for one source or another. Some stuff was just warmup writing or writing that isn't really quite about one thing or another.

Remove what you don't want and let the surviving material shine.

keeping cut Material

When I am revising a novel, I make several passes through, adding and removing material as I go. Some of the material I simply delete. Some of the time, particularly when I am not 100% on what the repercussions of the deletion will be, I remove it from the manuscript and put it in a separate file which is basically a scrapbook of all the material I chose to cut and keep. I tell myself that I may want to look back through this material, and it is wise to keep it in the event that I want to comb through it and reintroduce it to the main draft.

It might turn out that this material is needed somewhere else in the story. Sometimes it happens that way, and a simple cut and paste saves the day. Most of the time, though, this material just stays in the "cuts" file, very much like deleted scenes in a movie. It isn't always clear in the moment whether something might be useful in a week or a month.

The cuts file is a place where I can store my killed darlings, removing them from the actual manuscript but not obliterating them for all time. Like most writers, my personal tendency is to get attached to things, nostalgic about funny things a character might say or interesting turns of phrase. Even though they aren't right for the story, I'm not ready to let them go. So, the "cuts" file is a useful purgatory for this material, an icebox where bits of text can sit like dogs in a pet store window indefinitely wagging their tails and waiting for someone to come by and adopt them.

So basically, it's good to know your tendencies. If, like me, you tend to be overly nostalgic rather than a ruthless cut-and-rewriter, it's better that you put the material elsewhere. That way, you still feel like you kept it, but it's not clogging up your draft.

If you make the habit of trying to keep everything in your manuscript, you are training yourself to invite fear into your work. Fear, perhaps, that you aren't building skill. The more you freewrite and hone your process, the more you are right to have confidence in your ability. You can trust your spontaneity and gut sense more and more. If you deleted some idea that might have eventually blossomed into a winning idea, that's OK.

Yes, maybe that page was really good, and maybe if you had saved it, and chanced upon it at the right time in the future, you could have made something of it.

However, it's possible that the same good idea can reappear for you in the future. What is stopping you from spontaneously landing on the same basic idea again? Many people have had the experience of inventing something independently that turned out to already be in existence, only they hadn't been aware of it. It is possible for you to have the same good idea again in the future. If it is truly your idea, it's bound to find you again.

I have had the experience many times where I worked on a document to develop a scene for a novel when, due to some mistake, my new material got deleted. So I rewrote what was missing, terribly worried about the loss.

On more than one occasion I have come across a mysteriously restored and intact copy of the draft which included the material that I rewrote. In every case I found that what I wrote the second time was not only very similar, but in many ways better, more streamlined, than the first draft.

There are stories of authors who had carelessly lost their only manuscript to a fire or a hard drive failure only to set out and write the thing anew. I have heard from several of these authors. They also had little doubt that the second time around the draft was better than it could have possibly been before.

It's not a situation I personally hope to find myself in due to the sheer work it takes. But the lesson rings very true. It's safe to let old material go. Do so from a space of self-trust and a love of the process.

Freewriting Synergies

Freewriting, as you have seen, can manifest in all sorts of forms. Let's explore a few other ways of customizing freewriting.

Channel the Flow

Freewriting is about writing without stopping, allowing anything to come. You can tweak this by deciding in advance some different categories, modes, or topics you will freewrite about. For example, maybe you want to harness the strengths of freewriting to explore your goals and envision a better future for yourself. Each freewriting session you do, you intend to write about your goals and your future. Step one is to flow and see what happens. At times you will be on topic and other times you won't. But because you have geared your intent into a given topic, at some point you'll end up writing within one of your chosen categories.

The directive is that you honor the spirit of the endeavor, allowing anything at all to show up, while at the same time honoring your decision to write within this category. This means you do a bit of navigation as you write, holding the category in the background.

Whether freewriting within a category or not, the directive is to follow the moment. When writing in a category, you do both. Honor the moment, and honor the directive.

No Time Constraint

Ordinarily, you include a duration in the parameters of your freewrite. Maybe that's twenty minutes or maybe it's three. If you're crazy like me, it might be several hours. The rule you hold yourself to is to honor that time. Within this span of time, you have agreed to take the helm of SS Freewrite. You'll reach the opposite shore not by writing the correct thing but by flowing with the flow of language until your time is up. Having a time constraint brings an impetus and energy to your practice. You can accomplish a lot when you realize that you have a limited amount of time.

On the other hand, freewriting without a time constraint can feel more "free." You can write for however long you choose, and as you do so, you will write freely, without stopping, honoring the creative impulse. You can go do something else when the mood strikes. Then, when you return, you can simply resume freewriting again.

You hold yourself to the other rules of freewriting (no criticism, no looking back, no stopping, etc.) as if there is a time constraint, but there isn't. You write until something else happens. Either until your kids come home, or until you finish your piece, or until you arrive at clarity around your idea. Why would you choose to do this?

If you don't know how much time you have. If you want to write until you don't feel like it anymore, or until you arrive at clarity around an idea, or you need to write until you finish your article.

What to avoid: Muddying the waters of the practice.

OK, it's your life, so you do whatever you want with the technique. But there is a danger to watering down a technique. Here's what that might look like.

You like the stuff you have come up with in past freewrites. You want to freewrite some more, but you just don't feel like pressuring yourself with a deadline. Deadlines and time constraints are arbitrary, anyway, so why not write until it's finished? You write without stopping, but then you feel like slowing down, and then you sort of take a break, and sort of read back through and revise, and sort of write some more, this time more like normal writing. You write, you pause and think, you write some more. You're no longer freewriting.

I'm not going to say that freewriting is the only way you should be allowed to write. Write however you want. I personally freewrite a lot, but I don't freewrite all the time. When I want to write, I write. In my own process, there is a general urgency to produce the first draft, and so I am not critical, but creative, and I have learned that it is best to honor my impulse to write nonstop – when I want to write, I'm not going to do other things at the same time. I like writing. Basically, I have gotten to the point where regardless of whether I am freewriting or just doing normal writing, I follow the same philosophy. I do not always write to a deadline or timer. There are plenty of times when I allow myself to pause and reflect/reposition my flow because I am continuing to hold the overall vision and intent for the practice and not trying to force my way forward.

I freewrite because it's more productive but mainly because it feels a thousand times better. In my experience, my enjoyment and quality suffer when I divert very far from the basic fundamentals of freewriting.

Freewrite Through the Hard Parts

Yeah, you like writing, and that's why you're here. But like anything–anything– worth doing, it's not going to be pure ease and pleasure 100% of the way through. There will be sticking points. Sometimes big ones. And the tendency can be to avoid doing the hard work and instead keeping yourself busy with something else.

Let's say that you struggle moving past the world-building phase of writing a novel. An example of this would be if you love to explore the comings and goings of your characters. You love the feeling of your fantasy world. It's a real escape and it feels good to write and write and write. But in the back of your mind, you know that you're not only writing this for pure escape and pleasure. You also want this to be shaped into a book. You want to write it in a way that other people can enjoy. In the back of your mind, you know that you need to get your characters out there and into trouble. You know that you need to do some work plotting and pacing your story. And that doesn't feel as fun as just writing to explore the world.

So here is a suggestion. You can use timed freewriting sessions to explore the plot and story dynamics. Then, once you have a good scaffolding and sense of high-altitude story structure, you have all the excuses in the world to get back to writing and writing. Your meandering explorations of the world will naturally start to flow with a sense of direction because you know how everything fits together.

Module Recap

This module brought the exercise at the heart and center of deep freewriting: the writing marathon.

We looked at ways to outmaneuver stuckness and introduce variety into your writing with the turning a phrase exercise.

A host of tricks and tools is now in your bag of tricks so that you are abundant with resources that keep you flowing and focused.

Mainly, the focus of the techniques in this module was on how to really own the act of writing without stopping by bringing in various organizational tools and modalities.

Module 6: Revisiting, Revising, and Your Voice

First off, let me state the obvious. You're in module six! Things are really – really – starting to happen. You've had your share of ups and downs, and you have made it nearly to the conclusion.

For you, freewriting is way more than a simple technique for a single bout of writing. You're adopting a habit. You're gearing in. You are committing.

Now is a good time to do a bit of reflection so that the path forward is as clear and powerful as possible.

Questions for Reflection

Before you started this endeavor, what was your sense for how things would look this close to the end?

This question invites you to lay out any preconceived notions or expectations for your journey with deep freewriting. Maybe you were aware of what you expected, and maybe not. The path that gets trod feels very different from the merely conceptual one.

How does it feel where you are now?

What specific things do you feel you have achieved?

Many people will look back and see all the writing they have accomplished. Quite possibly, it is more sheer writing than you may have done before in a given span of time.

How has your outlook changed about writing, yourself, and any goals you would like to manifest?

What are you still most challenged by?

It's fair to say that there will always be challenges. One of the most empowering things we can do at any time is decide how we will orient ourselves with regard to life circumstances. Hopefully, in addition to giving you techniques and an invitation to rethink common beliefs about writing, you're feeling more confident in your ability, trusting the process, and coming to know yourself better. From an empowered standpoint, there's no harm in looking out at what you feel most challenged by. You don't have to be good at everything.

What would you like to get better at?

What do you still struggle with?

Revising Strategies

Revision brings the opportunity to re-see and re-experience your words.

For the time being, you're done writing. You're no longer occupied with the flow of creation. Now, you can take a more stepped-back perspective, assessing the results of your writing session. The wildness and madness and chaos has been concluded for a time.

From these flows, language has been made manifest. Even if it's not necessarily well-ordered, it has been given some sort of structure. It exists in the material world now.

From this vantage point, you can lift the language from its fixed location back into chaos to see new potential. This means holding the words in a space of new possibility.

Maybe, for example, if you cut a few phrases from your essay, they can find new life as a poem.

Revision is often (mistakenly) seen as a time of drudgery, a necessary evil, a time to cross things out and berate your prolific flights. A time to correct the many mistakes made during the reckless abandon of writing freely. But such beliefs about revision simply invite the tyranny of the mundane. So be wary of the unconscious shifts you may be making as you move from creation into revision.

Instead of handing everything over to negative beliefs that are anxious to clean up any messes, see what happens when you choose to continue to honor the mystery of the imagination.

How can your critical voice become the friend of the creative?

Now that the creative is sitting in the back seat, how does your critical side want to shine in truth?

Your Natural Voice

When you write from your natural voice, your reader can really feel you.

Your natural voice is the only one that matters, the only voice anyone should be striving for. So much about the way we learn to write unintentionally encourages us to write correctly rather than write how we ourselves naturally communicate.

Writing is an interface between self and other. Deep freewriting is all about bringing you more into your own unique and valuable way of experiencing the flow from self to other.

Nothing special needs to happen for you to write from your natural voice. Practice hones this skill, the skill of being transparent. It happens when you stop trying to artificially shape your language as if it needs to be another way. On the one hand, this sounds easy. The truth of the matter is that we have a great deal of deconditioning to do before we can write from our natural voice with ease and confidence.

What if your natural voice sucks?

That's the fear. My real voice sucks! I'm too ordinary, too boring, too something else, etc.

Nobody's natural voice sucks.

That fear keeps people in imitation, insisting on different styles. There's nothing wrong with imitation if you can discern yourself from what you are imitating. The problem here is that we generally move unconsciously from one imitation to the next. It can be very subtle, but perhaps you sense what I mean.

Some people insist on never hearing their recorded voice because it sounds different than it does inside their head. Some people can only allow themselves to be photographed from the left side. Plenty of writers will never allow themselves to get very close to their real voice.

What do I mean by real voice?

It's nothing magical. It is in fact very ordinary.

There's no trophy for when you begin to write in your real voice. But the more you do, the easier writing feels. It feels more direct. Clean. Transparent. It can come right out onto the page without having to be contorted and shaped and improved upon. You don't have to think about your words. You don't pre-shape your language, thinking of the right words or the best order.

One of the requirements of freewriting is that you be patient with yourself. You're going to be reading a lot of your own writing. The stuff that isn't true to you will probably get annoying. It will grate on your ears like a false note.

That might sound like a judgment, but it's not a negative criticism. It comes from a desire to move into authenticity.

Maybe you notice that you slip into a professional mode when you write, and it starts to grate on your nerves. Maybe you find that you tend to write in a kind of industry jargon that wouldn't easily connect with most readers.

I remember one writer at a retreat who struggled with his own writing because he didn't like the portrait it painted of him.

It's so convoluted and indirect, like Henry James, maybe – my writing, my voice, I find that it's not something that I enjoy. Which is not to say that I don't find some enjoyment in Henry James. Oh, I guess it is a general lack of decisiveness or... what's the word? Directness? Maybe directness... or something.

That's my little imitation of him. His revision brought out the distinction that there was a side of him that he wanted to work on. He knew that he had a certain side to him, the Henry James side, and that it wasn't really palatable for him at a deeper level.

That's what revision is for.

But also, that's what freewriting is good at. The more you return to it, the more your writing refines itself. You'll feel what it feels like to write in that voice for extended periods of time. The wisdom of the body and of your own sense of self's sense of inner gravity will bring you naturally and inexorably more towards what is palatable for you long term.

You'll get tired of the artificial ways you use to shape yourself. That's good. Because you'll also get fueled by your efforts. Don't merely brace against the strain and disgust. Learn from the disgust. Listen to what the inner critic is really feeling. Not what it thinks, but what it deeply knows.

Use Imitation to Feel For Yourself

Try this: revise your own work for awhile, then read a few pages by a writer you really enjoy. After a page or two, just enough to get into the feel of their voice, return to your writing. You're not editing to change your voice so that it's like that of John Steinbeck or Herman Melville or whoever, but you are letting yourself be influenced by what you already are influenced by, letting it contrast with what you feel uncertain about in your own voice.

Through osmosis, by letting them coexist with each other, you will find that not only will your voice be able to come to the forefront, but you will feel more vim for doing it, more steam for revision. And you may come to like many things about your own writing that stands rightfully side by side with whoever you deem to be great. After all, it's just a voice. It's very subtle, but it's not magic.

There are things that you can do that no one else could ever do.

What parts of yourself would you like to invite and engage during your next revision?

Rewriting Strategies

Sometimes, the best way to improve on something you have drafted is simply to write it over again. After reading through the draft, sit with it a moment, feel back into where you were coming from, and write it again.

Below are some strategies to take when rewriting, though they can also be employed during a freewriting session when you feel stuck. You are certainly free to use these strategies when exploring during a freewrite or when writing something for the first time.

Rewriting, whether in the moment or after the freewriting draft has been completed, helps shake things up at the level of voice and can put a new face on something that feels stale.

Go From Telling to Showing (and Vice Versa)

Whichever mode you are in, try revising so that you say the same thing but in a different way. Showing is generally the underused one of the two, yet interesting things can really manifest some times when you feel bogged down by a flowery or indirect style. See what happens when you just come out and tell it directly. And then what happens when you show it – illustrate it – more directly than you could tell it. And so forth.

Bounce Distances

This is similar to showing and telling, but with a twist. It involves moving from near to far or vice versa with the narrative distance of your writing.

What is meant by narrative distance?

A very close narrative distance is where the subject being written about is felt rather than regarded. In this closeness, there is an immediacy and intimacy which reveals in a way that does not claim to ever be able to know the thing in totality. Only parts and glimpses can be known ephemerally.

On the other end of the spectrum is the aesthetic distance, where the object is regarded, appraised, assessed with more remove. In the showing/telling sense, telling is more distant than showing.

A closer distance enacts and embodies the state of the thing, and the latter imparts and catalogs and describes.

Develop an Outline

If you have a big glob of writing that spans a page or several hundred pages, it's useful to step back into the outlining phase to gain some perspective and find a more streamlined sense of order and pacing.

Outlining a piece of drafted writing involves feeling into what has been written and finding how things want to be secured in the structural sense. It's about condensing the writing and summarizing it, finding how one section is unique and how it flows into the next section.

How long should this outline be?

That really depends on how rigorous you want your outline to be. If you just need something brief to move you back into a bird's eye view of things, then your outline can be brief, only a sentence or so per section or chapter. If you need to get into the specifics and rework a messy or tangled story, you will want a more exhaustive outline that describes the significance of each section, how it relates to what came before and after, any relevant story dynamics or character insights, and the like.

But Before You Get Back Into Your Project To Revise It...

Even though revision is the phase where you want to be informed by the critical impulse, it's important not to get hijacked by the more destructive tendencies of overthinking things and being negatively self-critical.

So, don't start dry. Warm up by freewriting.

Freewrite about your goals for the project. Freewrite your memories – the good ones, especially – from when you wrote the piece you're next going to revise. Write about what you most believe in and want to honor about the project. Get yourself into a state where you feel good and constructive. Your revision will go better when you are feeling good than when you aren't.

When you warm up with freewriting beforehand, you not only get negativity out of the way, you also get yourself more lubricated in the sense that words are becoming more of your environment. To really go deep with something and be really productive at it, you have to become immersed in it.

Revision won't always feel perfectly natural. To make the most of your time, you need to re-familiarize yourself with the driving forces behind the piece of writing. Get clear on your aims, your audience, the overarching structure of the thing. Even a simple five-minute freewrite can get you in a good frame of mind. Then, with clarity as your environment, you can dive in.

Reconnect With Your Motivations

There are bound to be times when you would rather do anything than revisit a messy draft or try to finish a book. You may have a nagging sense of dread about opening the document and looking at the thing in all its humble tangles. Be proactive by freewriting beforehand and you circumvent being ruled by that heavy feeling of overwhelm and confusion. It won't change how much might need to be done to bring an end to your draft. Yeah, maybe your project will look really messy. Maybe things are scattered all over the place. Freewriting is an easy way to help you feel up to the task.

You can't simply tell yourself that you aren't going to feel overwhelmed. You can, however, decide to engage a different action when the feeling hits you. Take a couple of minutes beforehand and engage the flow. You can use this time to rewrite and summarize the project. That way, you have a bit more perspective from which to assess things when the time comes. This is helpful even if you don't remember everything perfectly. That's fine. It's not a comprehension exercise. It's more about feeling your way into things.

Freewriting beforehand engages with the spirit of the writing project that is there, ready and waiting for you to come and polish it, to apply your perfectionist abilities and make it what it was born to be.

Being With the Critical

If the art of the creative mode is to get out of the way, then you might say that the art of being in the critical mode is to get in the way. Not in the sense of being an obstacle, but rather to be present, decisive, grounded, realistic. To fully occupy the space how you wanted to.

When you change drivers and hand over the helm to the critical impulse, you get to step forward with all the nags and advice and input you were ignoring during the earlier phase. The creative isn't the only side of you that gets to have fun. The critical gets to revel in things like:

- Cutting.
- Letting the material go that doesn't serve you.
- Waging war on what isn't harmonious.
- Making difficult decisions that the creative churned up but wasn't able to resolve.
- Changing anything and everything.
- Rewording.
- Reordering.
- Thinking strategically about the overall shape and pacing.
- Asking questions that refine your material so that it packs a punch and honors the life of your words and your intent

The critical voice is not just a naysayer. Although the critical can be a naysayer, I hope I'm conveying how essential the critical impulse really is. The critical impulse gives intensity, force and dynamism to your writing.

How is Criticism Different from Judgment?

Judgment is closed. Judgment offers an appraisal that is final. Judgment says "this is how it is. It's good, it's bad."

Criticism, on the other hand, can afford something workable and living. When the creative impulse is at the heart of what you do, criticism is like your helpful assistant, offering information and input, perspective and insight.

Criticism does not drive the car. The critical impulse informs creativity, yet it doesn't generate material. It can only offer its take on what is already there. That's why criticism always comes later. Not because it's unhelpful!

Module Recap

In this stage, we have invited the critic in earnest and engaged its sharp helpful eye in the overall writing process.

This is a good time to do some deep reflection on the material that has emerged and how it feels to be where you are.

Revision was at the forefront of this module and a host of strategies are available for you to continue to find freedom in your writing and not be bogged down with some project you don't know how to resolve.

We looked at the aspect of voice and tried an imitation exercise to feel into other voices. Similarly, we examined the strategy of shifting narrative distance as a means to get everything situated and well on its way to being considered a polished final draft, something that continues to exude a sense of freedom and creative wildness.

Module 7: Deepening the Flow

Now that you have been practicing deep freewriting for some time, I want to encourage you to make it a regular and ongoing practice. To that end, I will touch on some of its core benefits and offer additional practices which can help to spread the technique into everyday life.

As a practice, deep freewriting accomplishes a lot. In the most general sense, it reminds your psyche of what it innately understands: it's intensely pleasurable to be in the flow state and it is also possible to grow your engagement with the flow state with practice. It reconditions you back into this more empowered inner configuration.

creative chaos Is Not To Be Avoided

Not every masterpiece is going to get birthed without making a big mess. Though this can be daunting, there are practices you can engage beforehand (such as high elevation mode), as you write (such as "trees from tens"), and re-reading strategies that can help you from falling into a pit of despair when confronting the results of an hour-long writing marathon where things didn't go as planned.

The regular practice of freewriting makes the creative mode more accessible no matter what the time of day it is or where you are. No more timidly waiting for inspiration to strike. Through regular freewriting, you form an intimate relationship with inspiration.

It's important to keep returning to the intention to write in a way that deepens your trust with the flow state.

As we've covered, criticism is by no means bad or wrong. It's simply unhelpful to be critical during the initial phases of creation. We tend to do this because we have been habituated to distrust the flow state, that things must be carefully, painstakingly filtered and pre-selected beforehand. Both are needed. The creative impulse empowers us to produce material that is true to us. Criticism gives direction and life to your creative ability.

Break Through Blocks Once And For All

You get blocked because you let your doubts take over.

Doubts can be fine unless you allow your doubts to keep you stuck. Again, merely having doubts isn't the problem. By changing the way you relate with your doubts, you can overcome them. It's not necessarily even very hard. You just need to pivot the way you see your doubt. Then your doubt can inform you.

Doubt isn't only an obstacle. It also has something to offer you. Your doubt is really just a distortion in the creative/critical relationship. When it is rightly positioned, your doubt can bring you good information. Maybe you have experienced this before in life: Something that seemed insurmountable suddenly got turned on its head. "I don't think I can write that. It's impossible because I'm a hack, and if I try, I'll probably just wreck my life and look like a total failure forever."

So, give your doubt some room to breathe. It obviously has some advice to give. It's your choice whether to act based on that advice or not. Decouple the feeling from the need to take action and simply listen to what is really there under the initial layers of fear and frustration.

Give yourself a moment. The spaciousness of being that you invoke to do this will very likely unravel some kernels of wisdom for you.

"Oh, I see now," you might say. "I can simply make this shift with my dialogue and that fixes it." It was a perspective problem.

When doubt emerges during freewriting, give yourself space to actually experience it. Don't let it hijack your trajectory, but acknowledge that it is there.

Failing to acknowledge your doubt means introducing some level of inner tension that is counterproductive to the easy free-flowing nature of the creative process.

Phrase the doubt as a question. Then engage with the question, or if it begins to feel insubstantial as you engage with it, see what happens when you just leave it for later.

Not all doubts are based in reality. Some are just strange atmospheric residue, beliefs floating in the ether. They're cultural conditioning, they're something you inherited. A habit of thinking, nothing more. Once you see it, you can choose to let it go.

Again, I don't mean to suggest that doubts are nonsense. Much of the time, they stem from inner beliefs we hold which are in conflict with some experience we are striving for. These doubts have something to show you about a possible choice or trajectory.

The doubt might be "I'm broke and I'm worried that I won't be able to get where I need to go." The question might be "Should I buy this new car, or should I wait three months, save money, and buy that used one?"

When you pivot your relationship with doubt during a freewriting session, it can offer you greater perspective and move you towards greater freedom.

The trick for being able to use doubt to your advantage is that you need to have the distance from these emotional and intellectual pulls so that you can witness them when they come up. With some distance, you can recognize that it is doubt, and you can shift your relationship with it.

Instead of blindly letting it influence you, you can ask it a question and it will reveal what it knows. Doubt is a form of wisdom that is wrapped inwardly upon itself.

Blocks Based On Limiting Beliefs

You might have the limiting belief that "it's not realistic that I can write a book in a month." I myself have held this belief even though I have written a book in a month on more than one occasion. Doubts don't necessarily listen to evidence, but it can be interesting to see how your doubts respond in the face of evidence.

This is not about overpowering your doubt or being a bully to yourself, proving your doubt wrong. Those techniques can work but tend to be only work case by case. By forcing it one time, you may well have to force it again the next time, and the next time. Sooner or later you're bound to want to give up unless you are able to get beneath the big doubts.

The thing to listen for here is whether evidence can actually inspire you and get you to feel your foundation, your oomph and can-do spirit. I'll give a couple of examples for how this is possible.

Let's say you wrote a book during Nanowrimo, national novel writing month, but you don't feel like that book was very good. So, your experience has shown you that it's possible, but not that it's possible to write a book that you feel happy about. If you simply forced yourself to write it anyway, it might turn out fine, even if you have no idea what you want your book to be about or who you want to write it for. You can put some hours into it each day and refine as you go. There are much harder dreams to actualize. A book is made up of words, sentences, and chapters. It's doable.

The very act of repeatedly engaging in it can bring some clarity about the endeavor and get you more in touch with your depths. But given what we know about the benefits of engaging the critical mode to listen to our doubts and conflicting beliefs, I recommend working smarter rather than working harder.

You can be strategic about it. Before you start drafting your book, put some effort into clarifying the idea for your book and the audience you want to write for. Not having a clear idea is no reason not to begin the process.

Once you engage the process, see if you can allow yourself time to explore the terrain. By becoming more broad-minded, you can discover more of a clear trajectory, one that works perfectly for you on this project.

Based on the main elements you have explored about this project, you have the perspective to see how the writing needs to develop. Then, you can focus all your time on those things and not spend any additional time on discovery.

Setting aside that phase, now you can be wild on generating material that fleshes out your project. Having a durable and adaptive strategy is brilliant because it makes the whole process more efficient.

It's important not to be too rigid about your strategy, because it's OK if you need to adjust small things or even if you need to shift everything around. When you follow the actual path you need to take to complete your writing project, it's the spirit of the endeavor that you honor, not only the rules of your strategy.

For example, maybe you want to start writing a fantasy series. You got hit by inspiration a few months ago and have been carrying around this vague idea for some of the characters and plot points in the book. Record what you know, record what you don't know, and go from there. Keep that high-elevation point of view and return to it periodically.

The more you write, the more things will be revealed to you. You have your goal, your map, and your deadline. Based on that information, you can know roughly what you need to do every day so that you can meet your mark by the end of the month.

Getting Beneath Blocks

Behind most writer's blocks are limiting beliefs. Whether that is doubt or a general malaise, it's difficult to change unless you can get beneath the belief and see it for what it is.

A block, by definition, wants to create the illusory safety of stasis. One way of nudging yourself out from a blocked state is to simply put anything down onto the page. As long as you are putting words on the page, you are making some sort of progress. Sometimes all that needs to happen to silence a block is to acknowledge the feeling and engage the process anyway.

The weird thing is that we tend to imagine that we are the only one who struggles with our blocks. We mistakenly believe that our blocks make us unique. They don't. Actually, everyone can experience basically the same kinds of blocks for the same kinds of reasons.

Many people have blocks about being able to write stuff that's good enough. This "good enough" block can be addressed by engaging techniques that help you discover and own your own unique voice.

Yet the block presses back to say, "Sure, I can write in my own unique way, and maybe I can even write something that other people will like, but it's all pointless because it won't be a bestseller."

And right there you can notice how blocks are good at basically one thing: getting you to stop and seek the safety of stasis.

Other claims made by blocks:

- "I don't feel nourished by my writing. I have to try too hard because I'm not a natural."
- "I hate my words. I'm not eloquent enough."
- "I can only write during the mornings or at night after the kids are in bed. Anything else is totally impossible and completely out of the question. Without my environment being clean, silent and perfect, I can't create the brilliance that I expect from myself."

If you want something bad enough, you can find a way to make it work. A simple shift in focus can start to make this happen.

If you are confounded by your fears of failure – your certainties of failure – your paradoxical assertion that success equals failure and vice versa – stop giving them the time of day. Remind yourself of what is deeper than that. This is, after all, something you really want, dammit, and you won't take no for an answer, even if the no comes from yourself. You have to get in touch with the part of you that is positively relentless. This is a necessary condition for greatness. If it really is a big goal and you don't want it bad enough, nothing can help you. That said, everyone is capable of the greatness that comes from being in their own depth. Blocks drain our energy. Make the choice instead to fuel yourself to become unstoppable. Tips for fueling yourself:

- Take on only a bit at a time. That way, you get to check things off the list more frequently. Give yourself a small success and larger ones can follow. Small steps can accomplish huge goals. Letter by letter, the best books have been written.

- Embrace chaos. Give your perfectionist something to do ... later.

- Indulge in the process. Follow your whims and intuitions and revel in the chaos of creation. Engaging the flow feels good, and when something feels good it nourishes you. The whole thing becomes a lot more interesting. Even if you're convinced that writing equals work, not play, you know that somewhere, somehow, you have the ability to derive pleasure in this process. Don't judge yourself for what you find pleasurable. Maybe what you love about writing will become next year's fad. Who can say?

Here is a suggestion that invites greater rewards, pleasure, and indulgence into your writing life:

Associate something completely unrelated to your writing project to what you're doing. Let your infatuation with that thing subtly influence your tone or subject matter, even if it's completely unrelated to your topic.

Let it stay deeply subtextual. Experiment with ways to infuse your writing with this infatuated part of you.

Maybe it's the part of you that wants to rush home and make love with your partner, or frolic naked in the rain eating chocolate, and you find yourself freewriting your tax strategy blog articles. Nevertheless, encourage those urges and impulses and fantasies to be present with you as you write.

You don't have to write about them. Just let them be there, and keep doing what you're doing. Write tax strategy articles with a newfound zest.

Freewriting puts you into a better relationship with the fountain of ideas that is ever-abundant and always available. You need to write a book? Freewriting has strategies for that. Need to reassess your life purpose? Freewrite, circling around your most core values and then when you land on several that are juicy and inspiring, freewrite downward into ideas and goals and plans, then freewrite that material into potential activities and tasks. Do you feel stuck with your relationships at work? Freewrite to explore your feelings and lay everything out, then freewrite to get beneath these dynamics.

And be sure that you allow yourself to receive the nourishment this writing offers you. Each sentence is a victory. Each minute spent freewriting is a success that brings you closer to your goal, closer to realization and peace. You are fulfilling what you set out to do. It's messy, it's chaotic, and you are proving yourself equal to the task. In the creative moment, the wildness is part of the reward.

Freewriting With Pauses

What? How can pausing and writing nonstop go together?

Generally speaking, they don't, especially when generating an entirely new draft of something. But as you gain more experience with freewriting and come to adopt its underlying principles as your own, pausing while freewriting begins to make sense, especially as a way of adding more material to an existing document, such as during revision.

First, the fundamentals.

The main philosophy of my style of freewriting is that you want the creative impulse to be in the foreground. What does this mean? As we have covered, there are two impulses at work (with deep freewriting), the creative impulse and the critical impulse.

- The creative generates material branches outward is expansive harnesses fertile chaos
- The critical cuts bad material sharpens your focus stops fruitless activity structures and reorders

Of course, this is an oversimplification. For example, creativity can be very focused and finely-grained, and to some people that might look like it could into the 'critical' category. That's OK. It's a decent working model. A working model is all we need to build whatever we want.

So, again, we want the creative impulse to be in the foreground. And we hold it there regardless of whether we are writing or taking a pause.

Why pause? To recenter, reground, and refamiliarize yourself with your project. Or if you are revising, adding material to an existing draft, it doesn't make sense to do a timed freewrite if all you need is a couple of sentences of additional description or some better dialogue in one section. In those cases, writing for twenty minutes without stopping makes less sense than freewriting for only as long as necessary, and pausing when you need to read the surrounding text or feel your way back into the scene.

It would be easy to misuse this terminology or to misapply it, to justify stopping during a freewrite by saying that you're "merely entering a passive phase." That's why I tend to introduce this concept later. I don't want to unintentionally invite writers to work against their own intention to write without stopping. If you made the decision to freewrite for twenty minutes, then hold yourself to that technique. If, on the other hand, you are writing normally on your own time, freewriting with pauses is a technique that can create a bridge so that the technique can become the way you write all the time.

Don't stop because you ran out of ideas are fighting with yourself get tired

It's OK to pause when you want time to feel your body, to breathe, reconnect with planet Earth need to read some extra sections of your draft to add material to it, as when revising

To review, it is possible for someone to pause and still be freewriting, provided that they remain passively in the creative mode.

Active/Passive Creative Modes

Just as there is a critical and a creative mode, there are further subsets within the creative mode. Namely, there is an active and a passive creative mode.

While active, I write without stopping. While passive, I hold the same creative flow, the same questions. I remain present in the imaginative landscape. And I pause from producing writing. I allow the momentum of the creative impulse to continue and to nourish me.

You mean it's possible to stay in the flow even when not actively writing? Yes, it is. Interesting, right?

Freewriting, especially when you feel it from the standpoint of its underlying principles, is a very versatile endeavor. For the sake of clarity, we could define writing without stopping to be 'pure' freewriting, and freewriting-with-pauses an advanced technique.

It is advanced because it requires the writer to have some self-knowledge and the discipline to call their own bluffs, mainly to avoid falling into excessive thinking about writing.

Freewriting is a system that improves our writing ability because we power through our blocks. We flow right over our limiting patterns. And once you have enough experience with it, you gain some familiarity with your own tendencies. Some writers have no problem at all writing without stopping, but they struggle with staying on topic, or writing from their own voice. They let themselves be taken over by the momentum of the practice and end up doing something like automatic writing. Other writers find it hard to freewrite because they desperately believe it is necessary to stop and hand over the reins of their creative process to the mind rather than remain fluid in the fertile chaos of the imagination. To rest by default in the critical rather than the creative mode. Most people have a stopping addiction.

Stopping cuts off the flow of inspiration and takes you out of the creative. I think of abiding in the creative flow as something like an investment. We learn about investing money that, aside from interest, time is the most significant factor. A given sum of money invested will grow exponentially if you give it enough time, through the magic of compounding interest. The longer you hold, the more it grows. True with index funds, true with deep freewriting.

Pausing is beneficial because it grounds you it recenters you it offers a soft repositioning of focus it is a way of engaging the flow without insisting on active forward momentum it is continually open to inspiration, receptive and still.

So then, just to be absolutely clear, how is freewriting-with-pauses actually any different from normal writing? It is a way of writing supported by freewriting's value system: honor the creative impulse. Only do one thing at a time. Move forward into uncertainty. Normal writing is a wildcard. Everybody has their own approach. Some writers may organically arrive at something roughly similar to freewriting-with-pauses if they have the right kind of discipline and devotion. Freewriting is not an especially complicated method of writing. Anyone can do it. And it is my belief that the more people who engage in freewriting, the more fun the world will be. Freewriters have more of their own uniqueness to share with the world than followers of any formulaic or reductive system of writing or idea exploration.

I have mentioned the importance of abiding in the creative mode: when you're freewriting to generate material, you need to be in the creative rather than the critical mode. But you might be wondering: What does that mean? How does this happen? What does it look like?

The short answer: It's a choice, a decision. Having the intention can make it happen.

You remember how cars used to have retractable antennae for FM radio? Turn the key in the ignition or press the power button on the stereo and the external antenna would raise. With the antenna extended, the reception was good and the static went away.

When you're in the creative mode, you have chosen to be receptive. Your antenna is up. Instead of insisting that ideas need to arrive packaged a certain way, you have chosen to engage the flow of what happens to be there for you. And it isn't always perfect. Part of what it means to engage the flow is to be fluid, flexible with respect to what comes out when you write.

Sometimes a good idea is right around the corner, but we don't realize it because we have some emotional stuff in the way. By freewriting, you can process through the emotional stuff and move forward.

When you're creative, you make yourself transparent. You aren't hiding your emotions or trying to make yourself feel a different way. You are working to engage a purpose and maybe you have goals, but that doesn't mean your emotions are only allowed to show up in a given way. Unprocessed emotions will continue to stymie you until you allow yourself to experience them.

Being creative means being real. Being real entails engaging what is actually happening for you. Many nuanced movements of mind and energy are happening at once.

Any given moment, anything might happen. You might know what you want to say, and you might be uncertain about it. Freewriting gets you to be present with uncertainty and ride it like a wave. If you allow the fact that you feel uncertain about what to say to cause you to stop and think, you fall behind the wave and uncertainty overtakes you. Flowing forward with equanimity, you ride the waves and enjoy the flow of language as it passes through you to your reader.

When you're in the creative mode, the art is getting out of the way.

You're in the creative mode when you're open to the flow of new ideas and inspiration. Most commonly, this means you're writing or drawing or actively doing something to generate new creative material.

This is the active way of being in the creative.

One of the more valuable skills is to hold questions in the background to help you navigate uncertain spaces. A good question will move you. When you notice that you are blanking out on where to go next in your writing, call upon your skill with asking questions to help reposition your awareness. A question like "what does this character really want right now" can open doors when you're writing a novel. "What do I want my reader to learn in this section" can clarify boggy sections of a nonfiction manuscript.

When you write, you engage your will to put ideas into words. Any ideas, whatever ideas happen to actually be there in the moment. It's writing, so you can always come back later and change whatever you want about it, so for the moment, honor the ongoing spontaneity of flow and stay with it, not wishing it to be otherwise. If you notice part of you assessing that it's not perfect, you can always ask questions to optimize your trajectory towards what feels more vital, more "of a piece" with your vision.

Just Turn Down the Volume on the Critical

Often, the critical voice comes in as a backseat driver. Maybe it's trying to be helpful and maybe it's not. The fact of the matter is that you, in the creative mode, are driving. The ideal isn't to make the critical voice disappear completely. You have your destination, and you want to take turns driving. It just so happens that the critical voice is often loud and brash. Learn to turn down the volume on that guy so that the constant chatter gets silenced. It should be your choice whether you listen to the critical or the creative. But I also don't want to demonize the critical. They're opposite sides of a coin. You need them both to get where you're going, but they have to take turns. So, instead of kicking the critical to the curb, turn down the volume on the guy. If you have the volume turned down to, say, 5 percent, then if he has something absolutely crucial to tell you, you'll hear that, without any of the other critical chatter bothering you.

The creative is always welcome. The critical is only welcome during the later phase of the freewriting flow, as when revising or rewriting. During this later phase, when you find yourself generating material, you are in the creative mode, though you aren't handing things over completely to new invention. That phase has passed, and you want the critical to be guiding the process towards the specific aim of completing and improving the project.

Staying in the creative without ever shifting more into the critical would make it difficult to ever finish a project because things would just continue to grow and spread and branch outward. So, in the later phases, it's good to honor new ideas that land for you but not at the expense of finishing what you're working on. Let's say, for example, that you're writing an article and you're nearly finished with it, and you have this amazing idea that really pulls your attention. Honoring the impulse, you write a bit of that material, then your critical impulse notices that this new line of thinking really doesn't fit – the article would need to be thoroughly revised to accommodate this new material. Well, it's fine for ideas to come to you, so we don't want to push them away. We don't, however, want to cling to everything that comes to us. Making a note of it should suffice. If you want, you can put the material that doesn't fit into a different document so you can return to that material later and have the option of expanding on it.

Reflection Exercise: Freewrite To Own Your Engagement With What You Have Learned

Use the power of questions to return to the material we have covered, explore the facets that you discover, and turn them over in your mind.

Use the flow of the freewrite to discover new angles and to stretch your ability to describe what you have learned.

Repeating information is a great way of getting it to soak in.

Some questions to guide your reflection:

- In what ways do I agree?
- How am I unclear or do I disagree?
- How is it different from how I have worked?
- What do I like and what do I resist?
- How can I do better or improve on it?
- What does it boil down to?

- If I were to explain it to someone else, how would I do that?
- How can I take this and make it my own?
- What am I most receptive to, and what might I want to explore more in the future?

The goal with this is for you to be totally real and sink your teeth into your own experience.

When you're done, you have a richer creative foundation to rest on. The future is brighter for it.

Spontaneity, Authenticity and Ownership

Congratulations for making it through! You made it this far, and that means to me that you stuck through it because you wanted to, because you saw the benefit and so I really am congratulating you for your achievement. It's been a huge bunch of writing. As you move forward with this new way of writing, you say "I can" to the universe, "I can" to yourself. Where before you may not have believed it was possible, now you trod the path and prove it to yourself and to everyone else. Greater things are already upon you.

Let your writing be an act of kindness to yourself. All too often we get caught up in the end result. Let your writing nourish you. Be kind to yourself. Strive for big things, and strive in a way that feels good.

Example Freewriting Recipes

Here are a few recipes you can model depending on the following factors:

- How much time do you have?
- What is your goal?

The One-Hour Article/Essay

You want to write an article and have a lot of ideas but don't know where to start or what to say.

1. 5 minutes: sketching
2. 25 minutes: write without stopping
3. 5 minutes: reread and make notes
4. 20 minutes: fill in the missing pieces, reorder/revise
5. 5 minutes: polish

Let the questions lead the way! Be curious and you can figure things out using freewriting.

Since you have one hour total, spend the first half hour in freewriting mode then the latter half in revision.

Spend the first few minutes of your freewrite doing whatever sketching necessary to help you make the most of your time. Depending on your project, you may want to devote more time to generation or more time towards refining your material. Get clear on your desired outcome. Who are you writing for, what are you wanting to write, and why? Anything you want to leave them with, any desired outcome?

After you have sketched some of the main highlights you want to address in your article, proceed, still in freewriting mode, working on the draft. Start wherever first occurs to you and keep going from there. Resist the urge to revise or reorder. If you want to change something about what you just wrote, rephrase it or write it again. Leave notes for yourself within the document that makes it clear what you are thinking. For example, you could put your {revised phrase} in brackets. Just stay in the flow.

Then, when thirty minutes is up, spend five minutes reading back through it, highlighting or making note of what was working, what you liked, what left you curious about. Anything that feels like fuel for moving forward.

Having a majority of exploratory writing that is completely unusable isn't a sin. It's part of the process. It means you're doing it right. Just extract what you can into a new section of your document (or a new document altogether).

Once everything usable has been extracted, reorder what you have so that it feels good.

Use the remaining 25 minutes of your time revising this into a finished piece.

As time ticks on, gradually ease into more of a critical mindset. During the final minutes, hone and polish things.

Alternate Recipe for A One-Hour Essay/Article

Try this recipe if you would like to discard the freewritten material and use the second half of your time to rewrite a new and improved version.

1. 5 minutes: sketching
2. 20 minutes: write without stopping
3. 5 minutes: reread and make a new sketch
4. 20 minutes: rewrite
5. 10 minutes: revise/polish

30 Minute Idea Clarification Recipe

Try this if your end goal is to clarify your thinking about a topic. By following this recipe, you will discard the writing but retain additional clarity about the topic you explored.

1. 5 minutes: write freely
2. 10 minutes: discuss your topic, debate your idea with yourself
3. 5 minutes: reread, noting significant passages

4. 10 minutes: write more, elaborating and elucidating, driving towards a final summary of key points and main themes

The overall idea here is to use the inherent meanderings of freewriting to your advantage, as if you are having a discussion with a friend, trying to figure something out.

The workflow gets you to meander, then review your meanderings, and write more, all without any expectation that what you write will be kept. This creates an atmosphere of ease and informality which is important when you don't have the foggiest notion of what you're trying to say.

Try it and I think you'll find it very helpful.

Your Own Recipes

What works for you?

Keep a list of your custom freewriting recipes, putting down the purpose, the time required (along with a detailed breakdown for multiple phases), and any overarching philosophy or strategy behind the recipe.

Final Thoughts

The Magic of Putting It Into Form, Rendering It With Language

One of the myths adopted by "stare blankly at the screen" writers is that ideas must be worked out beforehand. Most people feel a constant distrust of the creative process. It would all be so much safer if things could be sorted out and organized before being written down, since that would mean making no story mistakes, no pesky grammar errors.

This belief, I know from personal experience, is not backed by truth.

The truth is that everything flows better when you engage the process before you have the words in mind. When you freewrite, you direct the flow of language onto the page, where your ideas can find shape. If we only ever allow ourselves to shape them beforehand, it's a recipe for constipated ideas and frustrated writers.

When you engage the flow of language first, before anything certain arrives, it's like you unfurl a wide net for your beautiful ideas to land in. You make yourself vast and receptive, but also central, immediate, and grounded in the moment's doing.

It is an orientation of confidence. You aren't expecting your ideas to arrive perfectly phrased or in the perfect order. But they will arrive, and this is far better than sitting and thinking, which is really just another way of saying "critically pushing away the flow."

When you have words on the page, and you are actively searching and flowing, magic can happen far more easily. Yes, creativity is magic. It is mystical. Being able to produce creative things only requires that we pair our trust in the imagination with a workmanlike approach.

When you freewrite as a way of getting ideas, writing before you have the notion of what you're supposed to say, you nourish the parts of you that have faith in big ideas. You show your depths trust and respect. Being willing to write before you know what you're going to say means you are willing to take a small risk and reap very large rewards.

You want it, so you're setting out before you have something to rest your laurels on. You're an adventurer. Instead of using the critical mind as an umbrella that fearfully directs good ideas out beyond your peripheral vision, you simply unfurl your innate creative ability with language as an inspiration-landing net.

Language has a strong relationship with how we think and feel and understand the world. By honing our use of the power of language, we can better map reality, navigate our lives, have clarity, and live freer of limiting beliefs and stories.

The Writing Part of Freewriting

Freewriting is a way of getting to a more vital force beyond thoughts. If words are the symbols created in resemblance of thoughts and feelings, then freewriting is a practice that teaches the writer to swim in the raw currents of mind and imagination.

This terrain remains locked away to most people – even most writers – except in rare moments where they experience "flow." But it is well known to the freewriter. To venture into this mysterious land, the writer must abandon the familiar comforts of knowing what is to be said before it gets said. No fearful thinking in advance, because, after all, the imagination is not the domain of the mind.

To enter this space, the writer jumps ship from the blocked-up mind and learns to swim in wilder currents, away from the ordinary judgments and the locked-in certainties of the mind. Our normal patterns are to seek certainty and safety, and when we freewrite, there is no safety against creation's wildness. Anything can happen. You might write anything. The future is unwritten.

creating versus consuming

Now that we are towards the conclusion, I'm going to step up onto a soapbox. If you aren't interested, feel free to pass this by. It's only indirectly related to the subject of freewriting, but I'm including it here because it conveys something of the spirit behind my impulse to share this material with people.

We are in an age where many things are possible. Entertainment is all around us, and much of it is on-demand. There's more material out there now than ever before. We embrace more market niches than ever before. Television has gone from a few channels to a zillion channels to devices that run applications that stream video content when we say so. No more is our reading selection limited by what is available at our local physical bookstore. We can have near-instant access to pretty much anything. It is easier now than ever before to find something that you like and buy it. It's easy to be a consumer.

And yet, here you are, working on your ability to master writing. If I could, I would give you a hug or pat you on the back for being here right now.

Because consuming is both increasingly easy to do and becoming more custom-tailored to our individual preferences, there is a risk that people will abandon their desire to create in favor of becoming a passive consumer.

There's no doubt about it that people make the world a better place when they are more in touch with their creative selves.

The task as I see it is to unfurl the layers of conditioning and to allow who we are to be revealed as soon as possible. We are works in progress. Allow the layers to be revealed and to pass away as you follow your inner light. Just as you didn't communicate the same ten years ago as you do now, be open to your self concept shifting over time. Discovery means moving forward and also about letting go.

So be bold, be courageous, and most importantly, become more of yourself every day.

What does that look like for you?

For me, a good indicator is whether I'm deriving satisfaction in my work. If my writing feels like a slog, I know I'm doing something wrong. It's my approach that needs correction, not necessarily my writing.

At times, writing may feel profoundly difficult. But when a writer isn't finding joy in their work, then I question what they are seeking.

I believe we are here in this life to awaken and transform. Even an act as ordinary as our written communication can play a vital role in awakening and transformation.

What do I mean by awakening? Awakening means entering greater awareness of what before was in the dark, latent or suppressed. Freedom comes from awakening. Awakening means having more choice.

What about transformation, then? Just as the alchemists of old sought to transform base materials into refined ones, we do that with our writing.

First, we work to develop unrefined material. A rough draft. Nothing terribly impressive. Word for word, there might be very little worth keeping. Nearly everything might need to be revisited, revised, reworked. However, only when the rough draft exists do you have raw materials to transform. It's just raw material: we don't judge lead as if it were gold.

If you don't write anything, you don't have anything to work with. Even if you don't end up using what you write, you have engaged with the flow. You're developing your ongoing relationship.

Choosing What We Get Better At

Just as we get better at something we work on, we can get better at things that don't serve our ultimate aim. We all develop more and more eloquent and convoluted ways of delaying work, postponing or procrastinating. Ah, self-sabotage!

If your ultimate goal is to be able to present yourself on the page as you really are, you owe it to yourself to follow through. If you are writing for an audience, you owe it to your eventual readers.

Either you take action toward that goal or you take action against it.

Unseen magic happens when you do work that engages the realest and most courageous parts of yourself. Don't let any outside factor get in the way of that. Ultimately, I don't believe that anyone is ever truly, deeply fulfilled by having or achieving anything outside themselves. While it's crucial to strive for and meet goals and achievements, what finally matters is moving always towards greater integrity.

We're all familiar with the stories of successful and famous people who are not happy even though from where we're sitting we believe we could be truly happy if we had what they had. Maybe some of us can relate, and there are things that we have accomplished in life that we thought would bring us happiness, but we find ourselves wanting something more or different. More doesn't mean more from the outside.

Everyone's goals are different. The thing we have in common is that we want to put ourselves into our writing. The writing as a natural extension of who you are. I mean this in the simplest way: nothing fancy or abstract here. Your voice, your vision, your words. Most importantly, not yourself in isolation. Your words as a way of connecting with the imagination and with other people.

Your New Habit

You want to adopt deep freewriting in some form or another as a new habit. What will that look like for you?

For me, it's writing at least a couple of hours a day. That's not even a lot, by some people's standards. But I know that when I do that, then things fall into place really well for me energetically.

So, I don't make excuses or talk myself out of writing like I did in the past. I make sure that there is time for me to write each day, and I forgive myself when I'm not able to make it happen. For me, whether it's fiction or nonfiction, writing feeds a desire and a passion but also a calling. I honor this pursuit by taking regular action. It's part of my life's core vision.

What's your core vision?